"The book's formative examination of public relations practice in Israel and the United Arab Emirates is a pioneering holistic approach to cultural influence variables. Notably, authors have lived and taught in the UAE and Israel, adding an unsurpassable experience dimension. It is an essential course requirement!"

Pam Creedon, *Professor Emerita, University of Iowa*

"Relying on the Global Public Relations Framework of five sociocultural variables, this book analyzes organizational identity, reputation, listening, and engagement in Israel and the UAE. It adds to the body of knowledge in global/intercultural/international public relations and is a must-read for those interested in these topics."

Krishnamurthy Sriramesh, *Professor of Public Relations, University of Colorado*

Intercultural Public Relations

This book examines the intricate relationship between culture and public relations within the Middle Eastern context, adopting an interpretive, inductive approach to explore how various cultural dimensions shape the enactment of key public relations concepts. Using the Global Public Relations Framework (GPRF) as a guiding structure, the book analyzes the influence of political, economic, societal, media, activist, and organizational cultures on public relations in Israel and the United Arab Emirates (UAE).

The book first focuses on Israel, investigating how cultural factors influence organizational identity and reputation. The book then shifts to the UAE, exploring how cultural dynamics affect organizational listening and engagement among organizations and publics. By examining the dialectical interaction between local and global cultural factors, the book offers a nuanced understanding of how public relations is practiced in these diverse Middle Eastern contexts.

This book provides valuable insights for scholars, practitioners, and students interested in global public relations, intercultural communication, and Middle Eastern studies. It highlights the significance of cultural specificity in shaping public relations strategies and practices, offering a unique contribution to the field's understanding of public relations in non-Western settings.

Ruth Avidar (PhD, University of Haifa) is Senior Lecturer in the Department of Communication and the Department of Health Systems Management at Yezreel Valley College. She heads the Marketing Communication track and is a former PR practitioner. Her research focuses on digital public relations, interactivity, artificial intelligence in public relations, and digital dialogue and engagement. Her work has been published in leading journals such as *Public Relations Review* and the *Journal of Public Relations Research*. She serves on the editorial board of *Public Relations Review*, *International Journal of Strategic Communication*, and *Corporate Communication: An International Journal*, and is a recipient of the Berger Research Award for ethics and futurism in global strategic communication, awarded by the Global Strategic Communication Consortium.

Ganga S. Dhanesh (PhD, National University of Singapore) is Associate Professor in the Department of Communication at the University of Maryland. Her intercultural experiences in India, Singapore, the UAE, and the United States inform her research, published in journals such as *American Behavioral Scientist*, *Journal of International Management*, and *Public Relations Review*. An associate editor at the *Journal of Communication Management*, she serves on the editorial boards of *Business Horizons*, *Journal of Public Relations Research*, and *Public Relations Review*. A recipient of several research awards, she led Zayed University's partnership with the UAE chapter of Unstereotype Alliance, convened by UN Women, and led the first Global Capabilities Framework study in the Middle East.

Global PR Insights

This innovative series of short-form books provides a new forum to critically evaluate contemporary scholarship and global practice in all aspects of PR and communications. It aims to promote and provoke new ways of thinking, providing an opportunity to reframe public relations beyond traditional frameworks, reflecting new interpretations, emerging research, and insights from different fields. One goal of the series is to bridge the perceived gap between the "academics" and "professionals" in the PR and communications fields, and to introduce diverse voices discussing theories and practice in the global economy. The concise format (20-40,000 words) offers both new and established scholars an accessible and supportive opportunity for publishing and disseminating new ideas and emerging research.

About the Series Editor: Donnalyn Pompper is Professor, Endowed Chair in Public Relations at the University of Oregon, USA. She is the author of several books, has published extensively in peer-reviewed academic journals and also has 25 years of practical experience as a public relations manager and journalist prior to joining the academy.

Intercultural Public Relations
Insights from the Middle East
Ruth Avidar and Ganga S. Dhanesh

For more information about this series, please visit: www.routledge.com/Global-PR-Insights/book-series/GPRI

Intercultural Public Relations

Insights from the Middle East

Ruth Avidar and Ganga S. Dhanesh

Routledge
Taylor & Francis Group
LONDON AND NEW YORK

First published 2025
by Routledge
4 Park Square, Milton Park, Abingdon, Oxon OX14 4RN

and by Routledge
605 Third Avenue, New York, NY 10158

Routledge is an imprint of the Taylor & Francis Group, an informa business

British Library Cataloguing-in-Publication Data
A catalogue record for this book is available from the British Library

ISBN: 978-1-032-43670-8 (hbk)
ISBN: 978-1-032-43671-5 (pbk)
ISBN: 978-1-003-36836-6 (ebk)

DOI: 10.4324/9781003368366

Typeset in Times New Roman
by Newgen Publishing UK

Contents

1 Introduction

Toward a holistic approach to intercultural public relations

Ganga S. Dhanesh and Ruth Avidar

Abstract

Despite the historical origins, growth, and maturity of public relations practice across the world, public relations research and education continue to be dominated by Euro-American centers of knowledge production with prevailing theories drawn from these specific cultural settings. This Euro-American dominance in research has led to the instrumentalization of culture, where non-Western cultural variables are often force-fitted into existing models that were not originally designed to accommodate them. The result is a tendency to apply Western theories—particularly those from the strategic management paradigm—to non-Western contexts, without sufficient consideration of how values such as individualism, democracy, marketization, consumption, and self-promotion might not translate universally. This introductory chapter critiques these shortcomings in existing public relations literature and sets out to offer an alternative perspective. It aims to set the tone for the rest of the book that provides a more nuanced understanding by combining both macro-level frameworks—such as the Global Public Relations Framework, which includes political, economic, and societal dimensions—and micro-level, culturally specific insights from Middle Eastern contexts. In doing so, we seek to offer a more holistic approach to intercultural public relations that acknowledges both global and local dynamics in contemporary practice.

State of public relations research across cultures

The practice of public relations as tools of persuasion to establish the authority of rulers and religious figures can be traced back to ancient

DOI: 10.4324/9781003368366-1

times across the world. Instances include the Rosetta Stone written by priests in Egypt to establish the divine rule of the Pharaoh, King Ptolemy V in the second century BC, or, a century later, in Emperor Asoka's edicts and the spread of Buddhism during the Mauryan empire found across modern-day Afghanistan, Bangladesh, India, Nepal, and Pakistan. However, the study of public relations as an academic discipline has its origins in the United States and Europe (Edwards, 2018; Garcia, 2024; Rechavi et al., 2024; Taylor, 2023). Despite the continued growth and maturity of public relations practice across the world, and despite the immense diversity of cultures and contexts that come into contact through globalization and the resultant production of global cultural flows through ethnoscapes, technoscapes, financescapes, mediascapes, and ideoscapes (Appadurai, 1996), public relations research and education continue to be dominated by Euro-American centers of knowledge production (Dhanesh & Avidar, 2023; Garcia, 2024; Rechavi et al., 2024; Taylor, 2023).

Globalization has been seen as an extra variable that challenges existing public relations theories that were developed to explain social phenomena within specific Euro-American cultural settings, often leading to an instrumental approach to culture, force-fitting diverse cultural variables as predictive variables into existing theories (Curtin, 2021; Edwards, 2018; Valentini et al., 2016). A recent review of public relations literature that examined public relations research topics and inter-cluster dynamics in articles published in *Public Relations Review* and the *Journal of Public Relations Research* from 2010 to 2020 found that although global public relations is one of the nine nondiscrete clusters in public relations research, the tie between global public relations and strategic management was strong, indicating that global public relations research often applies dominant theories from the Western-centric strategic management cluster to non-Western contexts (Zhou et al., 2023).

Since the 1990s, the dominance of Western-centric theories, such as the Excellence Theory (Grunig, 1992), has led to the development of various models and metrics that tried to globalize and simplify public relations research and practice and provide normative ways, benchmarks, and standards for global public relations, on the assumption that Western public relations theories are transferable to other contexts (Edwards, 2018; Taylor, 2023). Halff and Gregory (2013) have challenged the search for global public relations models and called for "a scholarship and a practice that embraces divergence and resists the temptation to converge, simplify, and generalize" (p. 418), since "diversity will be a mark of both strength and a reflection of reality as the practice of public relations develops around the world" (p. 418). For instance, Pompper and Adae (2022) critiqued the lack of attention to public relations across the African continent and argued for attending to indigenous cultures' ancient philosophies.

Attempting to develop a middle-ground theory between cultural relativism, which maintains that public relations must be practiced differently in each society, and ethnocentrism, which maintains that a single overarching theory developed in one society is suitable for all societies, Vercic et al. (1996) used the 14 characteristics for "excellent public relations" to identify nine generic principles that could be helpful to organizations practicing global public relations if localized to five specific environmental variables. Later, Sriramesh and Vercic (2003) introduced the Global Public Relations Framework (GPRF), which defined culture broadly to include political, economic, societal, media and activist cultures, arguing for the importance of simultaneously exploring the influence of these variables on public relations practice and theorizing in the environments in which they are embedded.

However, scholars have argued that extant global public relations theorizing reflects Western values, particularly the underpinning ideologies of individualism, democracy, dialogue, marketization, consumption, and self-promotion, which might not automatically transfer to non-Western contexts (Dhanesh & Avidar, 2023; Edwards, 2018; Valentini et al., 2016; Zaharna, 2016). Scholars have critiqued that even when global public relations theorizing might hold space for local aspects of culture, it tends to reduce the complexity of global public relations practices into predefined, often nationally based, categorizations of cultures and publics such as those offered by Hofstede (Bardhan & Weaver, 2011; Curtin, 2021; Valentini et al., 2016). Similarly, the prevalence of U.S. public relations textbooks in public relations education across the world exerts "epistemic imperialism that suppresses local meanings and realities" (Bardhan & Weaver, 2011, p. 6). Further, scholars have problematized the functionalist, normative, management-centric tendencies of public relations research and have urged dislodging public relations from its prime position as the guardian of Western modernist, functionalist ideologies and instead demand that public relations do the difficult work of representing marginalized, subaltern voices from diverse regions of the world (Pal & Dutta, 2008; Edwards, 2018; Rechavi et al., 2024; Valentini et al., 2016).

These critical perspectives highlight the importance of recognizing and embracing the diversity and complexity arising from cultural and identity differences. As a result, there has been a call for research that examines culture from the bottom up (Bardhan & Weaver, 2011; Curtin, 2021; Edwards, 2018; Pal & Dutta, 2008). Scholars have called for enhancing critical/cultural, interpretive, and postmodern approaches to global public relations theorizing that consider public relations as playing a significant role in the social construction of reality through exerting symbolic power, and that interrogate the role of power in global contexts of practice (Bardhan & Weaver, 2011; Pal & Dutta, 2008). The critical turn in global public relations research posed a fundamental question: should public relations be a conduit for the spread of Western, modernist ideologies in service of transnational capital, similar to casting a snow-white blanket across the world; or should public relations be used to highlight and amplify diverse locally-situated voices, especially those of the marginalized, similar to co-creating a quilt? The critical turn in understanding public relations across cultural contexts argued for a dialectical stance that embraces diverse perspectives and values and traverses the tensions between the local and the global (Bardhan & Weaver, 2011; Edwards, 2018). Some of these alternative perspectives include postmodernism (Holtzhausen, 2011), critical modernism (Pal & Dutta, 2008), and postcolonialism (Dutta & Pal, 2011).

Advocating a postmodern approach to public relations across the world, Holtzhausen (2011) argued that generic public relations practices do not apply since all practices are local within the postmodern approach. Instead, situated within the postmodern approach, which respects differences and is comfortable living with contradictions and complexities, Holtzhausen (2011) advocated for the emancipatory potential of public relations practice in international contexts enacted through various resistance strategies when faced with injustices and inequalities, foregrounding stakeholders' voices, and encouraging dissensus over consensus. However, Pal and Dutta (2008) argued for a critical modernist approach that straddles the critical and postmodern approaches by supporting most of what critical and postmodern scholars have been arguing for, but merges the interrogation of power embedded in social structures and the rejection of a grand meta-narrative or a singular truth, instead giving primacy to locally constituted discursive understandings of public relations practice that are also intertwined with global flows. Later, based on a postcolonial critique of processes of globalization and the public relations practices within these processes, Dutta and Pal (2011) offered a culture-centered approach as an alternative theoretical lens for understanding culture in relation to global public relations, that leverages notions of culture, agency, and structure.

However, critiquing the critical–cultural paradigm, which could lead to "an overwhelming determinism that paralyzes actual practice" and the postmodern paradigm that "lends itself to a situational relativism that can be equally paralyzing" (p. 95), Curtin and Gaither (2005) offered a circuit-of-culture model that approached public relations "as a signifying practice that produces meaning within a cultural economy, privileging identity, difference, and power because of the central role these constructs play in discursive practice" (p. 110).

Following this extensive and thorough review of the literature on global public relations scholarship, we agree that the field must acknowledge and embrace the diversity and messy complexities that arise from differences among cultures. There is no one excellent way of practicing public relations, just different ways. Building scholarship on these diverse ways of practicing public relations can strengthen the field and more accurately reflect the maturity and growth of public relations across the world.

Accordingly, we decided to examine the impact of culture on public relations in the Middle East employing a holistic theoretical framework that connects both the macro focus of the GPRF and a micro focus on attending to influential variables relevant to local cultures. While the plethora of alternative theorizations of public relations includes macro-level critical-cultural and post-colonial approaches and more micro-level postmodern approaches, in this book we aim to adopt a holistic approach that straddles both the macro and the micro approaches by (a) adopting the macro variables of the GPRF including political, economic, societal, organizational, media, and activist cultures, while (b) delving into micro cultural variables indigenous to the Middle Eastern countries we are examining in this book, to offer insights into intercultural public relations that are closely situated within global and local contexts of practice.

When exploring articles published in leading public relations journals from the last decade, we found many examples of studies that embrace multicultural perspectives, comparing public relations practices in Western and non-Western countries (Fifka et al., 2018; Vollero et al., 2022). However, there is limited research on the ways in which cultural factors influence and shape the enactment of key concepts in public relations literature. For example, how does *wasta* (an Arab cultural norm of preferring relatives and family when hiring for jobs or approaching governmental offices) affect the enactment of engagement or dialogue? This book aims to close this gap by exploring how cultural factors influence the enactment of key public relations concepts in the Middle East.

We chose to examine the Middle East for a few important reasons. First, the region has deep historical significance, being the cradle of some of the world's earliest ancient civilizations, cultures, and empires. It produced the first system of writing and is the birthplace of three main world religions. Second, the modern Middle East produces a substantial share of global oil output and thus wields much geopolitical strategic influence. Third, although there are continuing conflicts in multiple countries in the Middle East, the region has also witnessed remarkable economic growth, especially in the countries of the Gulf Cooperation Council (GCC), such as Saudi Arabia and the United Arab Emirates (UAE). Finally, significant cultural similarities and differences among and within the diverse countries in the region foreground the need to examine the complex influence of culture on the practice and theorizing of public relations in the region (Dhanesh & Duthler, 2019a).

Purpose of this book

This book aims to adopt an interpretive, inductive approach to examine the influence of culture on public relations. Culture is defined broadly and comprehensively as political, economic, media, activist, societal, and organizational cultures. We use the GPRF not to empirically test its predictions, but as a broad framework within which we will inductively examine dialectical movements between the local and the global, highlighting the influence of culture-specific factors on the practice of public relations in the Middle East.

Definitions

Despite the long history of public relations across the world, the field struggles with defining public relations practices within and beyond national borders. Terms such as global public relations, intercultural public relations, and international public relations are often used interchangeably, although some scholars delineate differences among the three. Intercultural public relations typically refers to interactions among organizations and publics across cultures within or outside of national boundaries. Ni et al. (2018) defined an intercultural approach to public relations as "how individuals and entities with dissimilar cultural identities interact and negotiate to solve problems and reach mutually satisfying outcomes" (p. 7). On the other hand, international public relations refers to the crossing of national borders. "International public relations are strategic communication activities performed in more than one country beyond an organization's country of origin" (Ki & Ye, 2017, p. 236). Global public relations implies practices conducted across the world, even beyond national and international borders. Although the broader term *global public relations* has become the predominant term reflecting the prevalence of business practices being conducted at a global scale (Ki et al., 2021), we chose to use the term *intercultural public relations* as we focus on the cultural contexts of the Middle East, which while harboring cultural differences also share commonalities. To examine the relationship between the unique cultural context of the Middle East and its influence on key public relations concepts, the GPRF framework will be utilized. The following section outlines the framework's key constructs, including political, economic, societal, media, activist, and organizational dimensions.

The theoretical framework: Global public relations framework

Political system

According to Sriramesh and Vercic (2009, 2019), strategic public relations practices are most effective in environments that support public opinion, particularly in pluralistic systems associated with democratic governance. Freedom House categorizes political systems into seven distinct types: democracies, democracies with restricted practices, various forms of monarchies (constitutional, traditional, and absolute), authoritarian and totalitarian regimes, as well as colonial and imperial dependencies, and protectorates. These classifications vary significantly in their openness to public discourse and dissent.

Notably, the 20th century witnessed a global rise in democratic regimes; however, a recent report indicated a regression in this trend (Freedom House, 2024). From 2005 to 2023, the prevalence of *Not Free* countries increased from 23% to 38%, with a decline in *Free* countries from 46% to 20%.

In the Middle East, the war in Gaza, which began after Hamas's large-scale attack on Israel on October 7, 2023, has further destabilized the already fragile region, where 93% of the population live under nonfree regimes (Freedom House, 2024). From a public relations perspective, the practice of public relations in the Middle East has traditionally served as a tool for governments to disseminate information about their activities (Kirat, 2005). The field has been closely associated with government entities, emphasizing traditional roles in publicity and governmental affairs. Scholarly investigations, including those by Albishri et al. (2019) and Sweetser and Brown (2008), have documented the efficacy of political public relations in shaping media narratives and influencing public sentiment.

Scholarship has also explored the deployment of propaganda and military public diplomacy by governments in conflict zones, particularly in Iran, Iraq, and Israel (Magen & Lapid, 2016; 2018; Sweetser & Brown, 2010). Sweetser and Brown (2010) identified that Iranian propagandists employed audience segmentation and targeting strategies to distinguish between domestic and international audiences, a technique paralleled in democratic settings. Studies on Israel's military public diplomacy (Magen & Lapid, 2016; 2018) have investigated the evolving nature of these efforts, revealing that the personal approach and demeanor of the spokesperson significantly influenced the balance and effectiveness of propaganda and public relations strategies.

Economic system

A nation's political framework is frequently intertwined with its economic structure. Generally, a pluralistic political environment fosters enhanced economic liberty, thus intensifying competition among market participants. This increased competition necessitates the deployment of strategic public relations to garner public endorsement and support. Conversely, in economies dominated by monopolistic public sector enterprises, the government often emerges as the primary audience for public relations efforts.

Since the late 1990s, the Middle East's major oil producers have significantly reduced direct state involvement in the economy, with an increased emphasis on private investment in infrastructure. However, the extent of this shift has varied significantly across the region. Countries like Morocco and Jordan, characterized by relatively higher political stability and rule of law scores, successfully attracted private investment, particularly in renewable energy. Nevertheless, the overall performance of Middle Eastern and North African (MENA) countries in attracting private participation in energy infrastructure remains poor (Somma & Rubino, 2016). Moreover, in many parts of the region, particularly in the GCC countries, partnerships between the public and private sectors are prevalent, often blurring the lines between government and corporate entities. For example, members of the ruling royal families frequently hold ownership stakes in private enterprises, merging private and public sector interests. This confluence of sectors has implications for the professionalism of public relations; for instance, research in Kuwait has shown that the degree of professionalism in public relations varies between the private and public sectors (Almutairi & Dashti, 2019).

Further, the composition of the labor force has implications for public relations strategies. In the GCC's principal economies, expatriates constitute 90% of the private sector workforce in Saudi Arabia. Conversely, in the UAE, Emiratis account for 60% to 70% of public sector employees but less than 5% of the private sector workforce (Durand-Lasserve, 2022). This division between nationals and expatriates across sectors presents challenges for public relations, particularly in identifying and engaging the appropriate target audiences. Significant research is required to elucidate how employee demographics across various sectors influence public relations practices. This issue is especially pertinent in the Middle East, particularly within the GCC, where organizations contend with a demographic structure characterized by a minority local population wielding substantial influence on major national issues, contrasted with a majority of nonnational residents. These dynamics have critical implications for the public relations strategies of governments, corporations, and nongovernmental organizations (NGOs), necessitating tailored approaches to effectively engage with diverse stakeholder groups.

Culture

According to the GPRF, communication both reflects and shapes cultural contexts. Since communication is central to strategic public relations, it logically follows that culture plays a significant role in shaping public relations practices. The framework highlights the dynamic nature of culture, noting the challenge of defining it given the hundreds of existing definitions. Within this framework, "culture" encompasses all societal attributes—political, economic, societal, activist, and media—while also referring to "societal culture," which includes values, characteristics, beliefs, ethnicity, religion, and other factors that define a specific culture. Furthermore, the framework incorporates "organizational culture" in organizational contexts, acknowledging the difficulty of distinguishing between the influences of societal and organizational culture. It also suggests that diverse societal or national cultures shape organizational structures through a varied workforce, fostering distinct organizational cultures that influence public relations dynamics.

Societal culture in the Middle East is influenced by significant ethnic diversity, including Arabs, Persians, Kurds, Turks, and Jews; religious diversity with Sunnis, Shiites, Yazidis, Jews, and Druze; and linguistic variety, ranging from Egyptian Arabic to Khaleeji Arabic. This cultural heterogeneity is particularly pronounced in countries with large expatriate populations, such as the UAE (88%), Kuwait (69%), and Qatar (90%) (Durand-Lasserve, 2022). The demographic composition of these expatriate population varies, encompassing large groups from India, Pakistan, and other Asian nations like China, the Philippines, Thailand, Korea, and Afghanistan, alongside smaller contingents from Western regions such as Europe, Australia, and North America. This multicultural landscape inevitably influences the practice and understanding of public relations, necessitating tailored approaches that respect and integrate these diverse cultural perspectives.

Extensive research has explored the impact of societal cultural variables on public relations practices in the Middle East. Al-Kandari and Gaither (2011) applied the cultural-economic model to international public relations, identifying Arab cultural values such as religious commitment, group devotion, resistance to change, attachment to history, and recognition of hierarchical order that shapes public relations activities in the region. Similarly, AlSaqer and Al Hashimi (2019) observed that in Bahrain, Islamic values and ethics, including relationship building, honesty, truthfulness, societal service, and community work, significantly inform public relations practices. Gaither and Al-Kandari (2014) further investigated the online communications of Islamic banks in Kuwait, noting a profound respect for religious authority aligned with public relations efforts, and suggested that public relations in Muslim countries would thrive under a personal influence model. This model, which relies on personal relationships and social connections known as *wasta*, has been documented as effective in various Asian contexts by Sriramesh et al. (1999) and is prevalent in the UAE (Badran, 2019) and Kuwait (Almutairi & Dashti, 2019).

Further, collectivism and group affiliation have emerged as pivotal cultural values in multiple studies on public relations practices in the Middle East. For example, White and Al-Kandari (2019) identified the collectivistic ethos of Kuwait, which promotes collective responsibility and social cohesion, as key factors enhancing cooperation between the private and public sectors, particularly in Corporate Social Responsibility (CSR) initiatives and in efforts to enhance the national image. Additionally, AlSaqer and Al Hashimi (2019) highlighted the importance of familial connections and social networks in establishing a strategic framework for public relations in Bahrain, underscoring the role of interpersonal relationships in shaping effective communication strategies. Similarly, FakhrEldin et al. (2013) argued that the region's collectivist culture, as opposed to the individualistic tendencies seen in Western countries like Denmark, influences the nature of networking and communication strategies, emphasizing family and community ties. Public relations campaigns that fail to consider these cultural nuances, such as those that are overly Westernized, often struggle to resonate with Middle Eastern audiences, as seen in the ineffectiveness of American-style media campaigns in the region (Al-Jenaibi, 2008). Furthermore, the role of public relations in the Middle East is evolving from isolation to globalization, necessitating a nuanced understanding of cultural differences to enhance outreach and engagement (Creedon & Al-Khaja, 2019). Overall, the integration of cultural values into public relations practices is crucial for fostering effective communication and building trust within the Middle Eastern context.

Research in the Middle East has also extensively explored the role of women in society and its impact on public relations practices. AlSaqer and Al Hashimi (2019) noted that while traditional stereotypes and gender roles continue to influence public relations in Bahrain, shifts in these perceptions are beginning to occur. AlSaqer's earlier study (2008) detailed the specific challenges encountered by female public relations practitioners in Bahrain, including cultural marginalization, professional relationships with colleagues, and broader social dominance issues. In the UAE, studies have investigated the multifaceted roles of women within the culture, economy, and public relations sector, providing insights into both the challenges and the evolving status of women (AlKhaja & Creedon, 2010; Badran et al., 2003; Creedon et al., 1995). Indeed, a recent study revealed that in the UAE, gender equality in the public relations sector is perceived positively by both male and female professionals, with organizations actively implementing practices to support gender equality, which in turn enhances employee performance (Lee et al., 2023). These studies highlight a dynamic area of inquiry, reflecting broader societal changes and their implications for professional practice in public relations.

Research into the intersection of organizational culture and public relations practice has shed light on how local managerial and organizational styles shape public relations methodologies.

In Israel, ethical practices among public relations practitioners on social media—such as publishing disclaimers for sponsored content, handling negative campaigns, and compensating bloggers—are closely tied to the cultural and social environment in which they operate (Toledano & Avidar, 2015). In contrast, Arab managerial styles are often characterized as authoritarian, patriarchal, and centralized, which have been linked to the prevalence of one-way and asymmetrical models of public relations (Almutairi & Dashti, 2019; Bashir & Aldaihani, 2017). This body of research underscores the significant impact of organizational culture on the practice of public relations, highlighting a tendency toward control-oriented communication styles in the region.

Research has also scrutinized various organizational factors that hinder the adoption of strategic public relations according to the generic principles outlined in the Excellence Theory (Grunig, 1992). These detrimental factors include senior management's lack of support for public relations functions, the exclusion of public relations from the dominant coalition within organizations, a predominance of tactical rather than strategic focus, insufficient formal research, and a preference for practical experience over academic qualifications in public relations roles. These challenges are evident across several countries, including Bahrain (AlSaqer & Al Hashimi, 2019), Kuwait (Almutairi & Dashti, 2019), and Qatar (Almutairi, et al., 2019). This body of research underscores the significant barriers that can impede the effective implementation of strategic public relations within organizations in these regions.

To summarize, a significant body of research on public relations in the Middle East has focused on analyzing distinct societal attributes, such as Islamic value orientations, as well as broader cultural factors like collectivism and the societal roles of women. Additionally, studies have examined aspects of organizational culture, including management styles and attitudes toward ethical dilemmas, to better understand public relations practices in the region. Collectively, these investigations aim to provide a comprehensive understanding of the unique and universal influences shaping public relations in Middle Eastern contexts.

Media

The interconnectedness of public relations and media, often encompassed under the term *media relations*, highlights the critical role of fostering relationships between these entities to promote organizational visibility and to supply the media with informational subsidies. The GPRF identifies three media-related factors that are particularly pertinent in shaping public relations practices: *Media control, media diffusion*, and *media access*. *Media control*, which pertains to the ownership of media outlets, is frequently tied to a country's political and economic frameworks, significantly influencing editorial independence. These dynamics are crucial for understanding how media environments affect public relations strategies. *Media diffusion*, or the breadth of media reach, can be constrained by factors such as illiteracy and poverty. Additionally, *media access* pertains to the degree to which various publics can disseminate their messages through media channels. The advent of social media has significantly influenced the dynamics of building and sustaining relationships between organizations and their audiences, emphasizing the importance of adapting public relations strategies to diverse media landscapes.

An exploration of *media control* in the Middle East reveals a spectrum of systems, ranging from *free* (e.g., Israel) to *partly free* (e.g., Lebanon) and *not free* (e.g., Saudi Arabia and the UAE) (Freedom House, 2024). Understanding these diverse media environments is essential for public relations practitioners operating in or engaging with the region. Despite the proliferation of media outlets, government influence remains pervasive, with much of the press under state control. This limits independent media and media training programs

(Swan, 2022) while often incorporating propaganda, thereby restricting the diversity and independence of news sources available to the public. These dynamics shape media consumption patterns, with a continued reliance on traditional outlets alongside a growing shift toward digital platforms.

Research examining the influence of media on public relations practices in the Middle East has primarily focused on operational models of public relations, agenda-building in political public relations, government propaganda, and media wars. Beyond the widely recognized personal influence model, commonly employed approaches in the region include press agentry and one-way asymmetrical public information models. These models, characterized by directive and often unidirectional communication strategies, have been extensively analyzed (Al-Kindi, 2019; Kirat, 2015). Significant attention has also been given to the role of information subsidies in agenda-building. For example, Albishri et al. (2019) conducted a study on the agenda-building effects of political public relations messages from the Saudi and U.S. governments during Donald Trump's visit to the Middle East. The research demonstrated that government-provided messages significantly impacted media coverage and public opinion, affecting all three levels of agenda-building. This body of research highlights the diverse strategies used to shape public discourse and manage public perception through media relations. Consistent with the view that the primary goal of public relations is to secure publicity and enhance an organization's image, media relations is considered a central component of public relations in the region (Al-Kindi, 2019; Kirat, 2015).

Media diffusion in the Middle East is shaped by a complex interplay between traditional and digital media, heavily influenced by social inequality and government control. A study of news media repertoires in seven MENA countries highlighted that social inequality significantly impacts how individuals access and combine different news sources, with digital media playing a crucial role in shaping these patterns (Leuppert et al., 2024). Indeed, the region has experienced a notable rise in social media usage, making it a market leader, with multiple countries ranked above the global average in terms of the percentage of the population using social networks, including the UAE, Bahrain, Qatar, Lebanon, and Oman (Go-Globe, 2024). Additionally, there is an increase in e-commerce on social media, influencer marketing, and video content. However, countries like South Sudan, where only 4.3% of the population uses social media, and Egypt, with 44.5% usage, remain exceptions to this trend (Go-Globe, 2024).

Regarding *media access*, research highlights the robust integration of information and communication technologies into public relations practices, significantly shaping efforts and transforming communication strategies. The use of social media in public relations enhances the interactive relationship between institutions and the public, underscoring the increasing importance of media relations in the digital age (Hassan, 2023). Culture-centered public relations models, like the *majlis* in the UAE and the *Wali office* in Oman, highlight how traditional structures can be integrated into modern public relations practices. The *majlis* provides a direct, participatory forum for public dialogue with rulers, fostering community engagement in a traditional political system (Badran, 2019). Similarly, in Oman, the *Wali* mediates between the government and local communities, while the *Sablah* functions as a meeting space for discussing local affairs (Al-Kindi, 2019). These models emphasize cultural sensitivity and inclusivity in public relations.

Despite the potential of social media to support interactive and reciprocal communication models, Middle Eastern organizations often primarily use platforms like Twitter and Instagram, as well as smartphones, for promotional purposes and one-way communication, failing to fully leverage their dialogic capabilities to engage with and build relationships with their publics (AlKandari et al., 2019; Avidar, 2015; Avidar et al., 2013; Bashir & Aldaihani, 2017; Storie, 2015). In addition, research in the Israeli context has highlighted questionable ethical practices in social media environments, linking public relations ethics to the cultural and social settings in which practitioners operate. These practices have been argued to potentially decrease the perceived trustworthiness of media and business organizations engaging in them (Lahav, 2016; Lahav & Zimand-Sheiner, 2016; Toledano & Avidar, 2015). In the UAE, Dhanesh and Duthler (2019b) found a positive correlation between awareness of paid endorsements and the strength of follower-influencer relationships. These findings suggest that while social media provides tools for two-way communication, dialogue, and engagement, its potential remains underutilized, reflecting a gap between capability and practice in public relations across the region.

In summary, research on the relationship between media and public relations practices in the region has explored various aspects, including public relations models, the agenda-building role of political public relations, and government propaganda. Furthermore, studies have investigated whether public relations professionals effectively leverage social media to facilitate dialogue, implement two-way communication models, and foster stakeholder engagement and relationships online.

Activism

A nation's political and economic frameworks significantly shape the extent and nature of activism within its society. Generally, democratic pluralistic societies and economically advanced nations are more tolerant and supportive of activism (Dunn & Singh, 2014). In contrast, in developing economies, activism may be largely confined to formal labor union activities. Historically, activists were often viewed as adversaries to organizations, posing challenges that required management through public relations strategies. However, this perspective is evolving. Increasingly, public relations practitioners are not only mediating between organizations and activists but are also becoming activists themselves within these organizations and actively participating in activist groups (Dhanesh & Sriramesh, 2019).

Despite the widespread impact of the Arab Spring across multiple countries in the Middle East and North Africa during 2010 and 2011, public relations research on the phenomenon has remained limited. However, studies have highlighted the role of social networks, both online and offline, in amplifying protests and enabling new forms of collective action, particularly through platforms like Facebook and Twitter (Al-Jenaibi, 2014; Allagui & Kuebler, 2011; Jamil, 2022).

The Arab Spring demonstrated the potential of digital technologies to empower citizens and disrupt authoritarian regimes, as seen in the widespread protests that toppled several dictators in the region (Zayani, 2019). However, the initial optimism surrounding social media as a tool for liberation has been tempered by the rise of digital authoritarianism. Governments in the Middle East, such as those in Saudi Arabia and the UAE, have increasingly harnessed digital technologies for surveillance, censorship, and disinformation to maintain control and suppress dissent (Cosentino, 2022). This has led to a complex landscape where social media serves both as a platform for activism and a tool for authoritarian control.

Despite these challenges, social media remains a vital platform for political expression and activism, as demonstrated by movements like the Israeli Social Justice movement, which leveraged these platforms to address social and economic issues beyond traditional political conflicts (Katz, 2019). In 2023, massive civil society mobilizations in Israel responded to illiberal constitutional changes and a subsequent war, marking a transition from protest to aid provision by organizations (Gidron & Katz, 2024). Protests against proposed legal reforms in the same year also evolved, with slogans shifting from concerns about a "legal revolution" to accusations of a "regime coup," emphasizing democratic values and appealing to international communities (Berenson, 2023). Together, these movements illustrate the multifaceted nature of activism in Israel, shaped by both local and international influences and reflecting broader societal changes. More broadly, the dual role of social media in the Middle East underscores its capacity to empower citizens while simultaneously being co-opted by regimes, highlighting the complex interplay between digital activism and authoritarian resilience in the region (Cosentino, 2022)

Beyond the realms of political protest and conflict, Allagui (2017) explored corporate public relations activism in monarchical settings. An analysis of award-winning campaigns in the UAE showed that public relations practitioners and managers demonstrated a commitment to social activism, which can challenge power structures and drive social change. In many Arab states, certain stakeholder groups such as trade unions and lobbyists face significant restrictions. Additionally, the status of local NGOs and charities often lacks clear definition and formal legal recognition. For instance, the Red Crescent Society in the UAE operates as a state-run organization, while other private charities frequently fall under the management of ruling family members, complicating distinctions between governmental and nongovernmental entities (Selvik, 2013). Consequently, there is scant research focusing on activism and NGOs in the Middle East, reflecting these complexities and constraints (Duthler et al., 2015).

Although this review has examined each variable individually within the context of the GPRF as outlined by Sriramesh & Vercic (2009, 2019), it is apparent that these variables are interconnected and collectively influence public relations practices in the Middle East. For example, the prevalent use of the personal influence model, press agentry, and one-way public information models in the region can be attributed to societal cultural factors like the importance of social connections, as well as organizational culture factors such as authoritarian management styles. Additionally, the studies on propaganda and media wars demonstrate how political and media cultures interact and jointly shape public relations practices in the region, highlighting the complex interplay of various cultural, political, and organizational dynamics in defining the landscape of public relations.

Chapters in this book

This book addresses four key concepts in public relations as practiced in two Middle Eastern countries—Israel and the UAE. It examines how the macro variables of the GPRF, including political, economic, societal, organizational, media, and activist cultures, as well as the micro-cultural variables indigenous or relevant to the countries studied, affect the enactment of these public relations concepts in these specific contexts of practice. Chapters 2 and 3 are set in Israel and examine the impact of cultural variables on organizational identity and reputation. Chapters 4 and 5 are set in the UAE and explore the impact of cultural factors on the enactment of organizational listening and engagement between organizations and publics.

Chapter 2 on the formation of organizational identity examines the impact of various cultural, political, and societal factors within the Israeli context. Specifically, it explores how Israeli organizations form their identities while navigating a pluralistic political system, rich religious and ethnic diversity, and a dynamic yet polarized society. By analyzing the interplay between internal values, beliefs, and external cultural factors, the chapter highlights the role of public relations in shaping organizational identity. It introduces the concept of *culturally grounded organizational identity formation* to describe the dynamic, co-creational processes through which organizations construct their identities in response to socio-political, economic, and cultural realities. Key elements include cultural integration, political and economic responsiveness, diversity, equity, and inclusion, and societal engagement.

Chapter 3 on organizational reputation explores the relationship between organizational reputation and cultural factors within the Israeli context. Specifically, it examines the influence of economic systems, societal and organizational culture, and the media system on the process of organizational reputation building. The chapter introduces the *culturally embedded organizational reputation model*, which identifies cultural integration and responsiveness, political and economic adaptability, media savviness, and co-creation and meaningful engagement with stakeholders as critical components of reputation-building. Israeli organizations are shown to align with values such as mutual responsibility, solidarity, patriotism, innovation, and entrepreneurship to address societal complexities and enhance their reputations.

Chapter 4 on organizational listening explores the impact of cultural factors on the practice of organizational listening in the UAE. Specifically, it explores the influence of being an economically vibrant federation amidst a geopolitical tinderbox in the Middle East, characterized by high-context, indirect, oral cultures in a melting pot of diversity of 200 nationalities, a highly calibrated media system, and limited appetite for activism. The chapter proposes the concept of *subtextual organizational listening* to the sounds of silence as appropriate to organizational listening in a high-context, indirect, oral culture with a regulated media system. Subtextual organizational listening is defined as organizational listening where communication is indirect and nuanced, often relying on unspoken or implied messages rather than overt speech. It reflects the idea of listening to what is not directly said, but is understood through context, tone, gestures, or shared knowledge, needed in high-context cultures with restrictions on free speech.

Chapter 5 on engagement between organizations and their publics in the UAE explores how features of a political economy led by a strong government, a societal culture predominantly underpinned by relational logic, and a media system that operates within restricted freedom of expression impacts the enactment of engagement. The chapter proposes the concept of *bounded relational engagement* defined as complex, dialectical connections among interacting entities that are grounded in close, high-quality, interpersonal relationships and networks of homophily, but are simultaneously constrained or hemmed by the inequities created by these hierarchical, networked relationships, as well as the legal, regulatory, and cultural frameworks governing freedom of expression and other boundaries.

The four chapters illustrate their arguments with case studies from the respective countries and argue that while the frameworks and concepts proposed are grounded in the culturally specific contexts of Israel and the UAE, they might also be applicable to other contexts that share similar characteristics. Each chapter also includes questions that trigger further discussion.

Our hope is that this book opens the door for further studies that examine how public relations practices across the world might be impacted by macro and micro variables of cultural influence and propose fresh perspectives on practicing public relations in diverse cultural contexts, reflecting the richness and maturity of public relations practices across the world.

References

Al-Jenaibi, B. (2008). The effects of media campaigns on different cultures. *International Journal of Humanities and Social Sciences, 2*(10), 1067–1070. https://doi.org/10.1504/IJBG.2013.056873

Al-Jenaibi, B. (2014). The nature of Arab public discourse: Social media and the 'Arab Spring'. *Journal of Applied Journalism & Media Studies, 3*(2), 241–260. https://doi.org/10.1386/ajms.3.2.241_1

Al-Kandari, A., & Gaither, T.K. (2011). Arabs, the west and public relations: A critical/cultural study of Arab cultural values. *Public Relations review, 37*(3), 266–273. https://doi.org/10.1016/j.pubrev.2011.04.002

Al-Kandari, A.A., Gaither, T.K., Alfanad, M.M., Dashti, A.A., & Alsaber, A.R. (2019). An Arab perspective on social media: How banks in Kuwait use Instagram for public relations. *Public Relations Review, 45*, 101774. https://doi.org/10.1016/j.pubrev.2019.04.007

Al-Khaja, M.A.W., & Creedon, P. (2010). Evaluating the effectiveness of the first breast cancer awareness campaign in the United Arab Emirates: Lessons learned and next steps. *Public Relations Review, 36*(4), 386–388. https://doi.org/10.1016/j.pubrev.2010.06.005

Al-Kindi, A.K. (2019). Public relations units in the Omani civil service sector: Historical background and current characteristics. In T.M. Almutairi and D. Kruckeberg (Eds.). *Public Relations in the Gulf Cooperation Countries: An Arab Perspective*, pp. 53–73. Routledge. https://doi.org/10.4324/9781351064989-4

Albishri, O., Tarasevich, S., Proverbs, P., & Kiousis, S.K. (2019). Mediated public diplomacy in the digital age: Exploring the Saudi and the U.S. governments' agenda-building during Trump's visit to the Middle East. *Public Relations Review,* 45(4), 101820. https://doi.org/10.1016/j.pubrev.2019.101820

Allagui, I. (2017). Towards organizational activism in the UAE: A case study approach. *Public Relations Review, 43,* 258–266. https://doi.org/10.1016/j.pubrev.2016.12.007

Allagui, I., & Kuebler, J. (2011). The Arab Spring and the role of ICTs: Editorial introduction. *International Journal of Communication, 5*, 1435–1442.

Almutairi, T.M., & Dashti, A.A. (2019). Public relations in Kuwait: A historical, practical, and theoretical perspective. In T.M. Almutairi and D.

Kruckeberg (Eds.). *Public Relations in the Gulf Cooperation Countries: An Arab Perspective*, pp. 31–52. Routledge. https://doi.org/10.4324/9781351064989-3

Almutairi, T.M., Galander, M.M., Al-Balushi, O.A., & Al Balushi, R.A. (2019). Qatar public relations: In focus. In T.M. Almutairi and D. Kruckeberg (Eds.). *Public Relations in the Gulf Cooperation Countries: An Arab Perspective*, pp. 74–97. Routledge. https://doi.org/10.4324/9781351064989-5

AlSaqer, L. (2008). Experience of female public relations practitioners in Bahrain. *Public Relations Review, 34*(1), 77–79. https://doi.org/10.1016/j.pubrev.2007.08.017

AlSaqer, L., & Al Hashimi, S. (2019). The status and new directions of public relations practice in Bahrain. In T.M. Almutairi and D. Kruckeberg (Eds.). *Public Relations in the Gulf Cooperation Countries: An Arab Perspective*, pp. 5–30. Routledge. https://doi.org/10.4324/9781351064989-2

Appadurai, A. (1996). *Modernity at large: Cultural dimensions of globalization*. University of Minnesota Press.

Avidar, R. (2015). Smartphones, publics, and OPR: Do publics want to engage? *Public Relations Review, 41*(2), 214–221. https://doi.org/10.1016/j.pubrev.2014.11.019

Avidar, R., Ariel, Y., Malka, V., & Levy, E.C. (2013). Smartphones and young publics: A new challenge for public relations practice and relationship building. *Public Relations Review, 39*(5), 603–605. https://doi.org/10.1016/j.pubrev.2013.09.010

Badran, B. (2019). A critical snapshot of the practice of public relations in the United Arab Emirates. In T.M. Almutairi and D. Kruckeberg (Eds.). *Public Relations in the Gulf Cooperation Countries: An Arab Perspective*, pp. 118–144. Routledge. https://doi.org/10.4324/9781351064989-7

Badran, B., Turk, J., & Walters, T. (2003). Sharing the transformation: Public relations and the UAE come of age. In K. Sriramesh and D. Vercic (Eds.). *The Global Public Relations Handbook Theory, Research and Practice*, pp. 46–67. New York, NY: Routledge.

Bardhan, N., & Weaver, C.K. (2011). Introduction: Public relations in global cultural contexts. In N. Bardhan and C.K. Weaver (Eds.). *Public relations in Global Cultural Contexts: Multi-paradigmatic Perspectives*, pp. 1–28. Routledge. https://doi.org/10.4324/9780203866153

Bashir, M., & Aldaihani, A. (2017). Public relations in an online environment: Discourse description of social media in Kuwaiti organizations. *Public Relations Review, 43*(4), 777–787. https://doi.org/10.1016/j.pubrev.2017.05.004

Berenson, A. (2023). Legal reform or regime coup? Three stages in the evolution of protest signs in Israeli social activism. In S. Serpa and D. Cameron

Kelly (Eds.). *Social Activism – New Challenges in a (Dis)connected World*. IntechOpen. ISBN: 978-1-83769-877-6.

Cosentino, G. (2022). Digital authoritarianism in the Middle East: Deception, disinformation and social media. *Bustan: Middle East Book Review, 13*(2), 190–197. https://doi.org/10.5325/bustan.13.2.0190

Creedon, P., & Al-Khaja, M. (2019). An overview of Middle East public relations practice, education, and research from isolation to globalization. *Journal of Public Relations Research, 31*, 84–96.https://doi.org/10.1080/1062726X.2019.1682324

Creedon, P., Al-Khaja, M., & Kruckeberg, D. (1995). Women and public relations education and practice in the United Arab Emirates. *Public Relations Review, 21*(1), 59–76. https://doi.org/10.1016/0363-8111(95)90040-3

Curtin, P. (2021). Public relations and cultural theories. In C. Valentini (Ed.). Public Relations, pp.563–580. De Gruyter Mouton. https://doi.org/10.1515/9783110554250-029

Curtin, P.A., & Gaither, T.K. (2005). Privileging identity, difference, and power: The circuit of culture as a basis for public relations theory. *Journal of Public Relations Research, 17*(2), 91–115. https://doi.org/10.1207/s1532754xjprr1702_3

Dhanesh, G.S., & Avidar, R. (2023). Culture and dialog theory in public relations: The Middle Eastern context. In E. Sommerfeldt and C. Botan (Eds.). *Public Relations Theory III*, pp. 321–337. Routledge. ISBN: 9780367683313.

Dhanesh, G.S., & Duthler, G. (2019a). Public relations in the Middle East: An editorial introduction. *Journal of Public Relations Research, 31*(3–4), 71–83.

Dhanesh, G.S., & Duthler, G. (2019b). Relationship management through social media influencers: Effects of followers' awareness of paid endorsement. *Public Relations Review, 45*(3), 101765. https://doi.org/10.1016/j.pubrev.2019.03.002

Dhanesh, G.S., & Sriramesh, K. (2019). The nexus between activism and public relations. In K. Sriramesh and D. Vercic (Eds.) *Global Public Relations Handbook* (3rd edition). Routledge. https://doi.org/10.4324/9781315173290

Dunn, K., & Singh, S.P. (2014). Pluralistic conditioning: Social tolerance and effective democracy. *Democratization, 21*(1), 1–28. https://doi.org/10.1080/13510347.2012.697056

Durand-Lasserve, O. (2022). Nationalization of the private sector labor force, quotas, matching and public jobs, an illustration with Saudi Arabia. *The Quarterly Review of Economics and Finance, 86*, 98–117. https://doi.org/10.1016/j.qref.2022.06.004

Duthler, G., Watson, T., Theofilou, T., & Sthapitanonda, P. (2015). CSR and stakeholder engagement perspectives from the United Arab Emirates. *Journal of Communication Arts, 33*(2), 48–56.

Dutta, M.J., & Pal, M. (2011). Public relations and marginalization in a global context: A postcolonial critique. In N. Bardhan and C.K. Weaver (Eds.). *Public Relations in Global Contexts: Multi-paradigmatic Perspectives*. Routledge.

Edwards, L. (2018). *Public relations and globalisation. Understanding public relations: Theory, culture and society (ch.7)*. SAGE Publications Ltd.

FakhrEldin, H., Skoko, H., & Cheraghi, M. (2013). The effect of national culture on entrepreneurs' networks: A comparison of the MENA region and Denmark. *International Journal of Business and Globalisation, 11*(4), 353–366. https://doi.org/10.1504/IJBG.2013.056873

Fifka, M.S., Kühn, A.L., & Stiglbauer, M. (2018). "One size fits all"? Convergence in international corporate social responsibility communication—A comparative study of CSR mission statements in the United States and India. *Journal of Public Affairs, 18*(3), 16–70. https://doi.org/10.1002/pa.1670

Freedom House (2024). Freedom in the world 2024. In *Freedom House*. https://freedomhouse.org/sites/default/files/2024-02/FIW_2024_Digital Booklet.pdf

Gaither, T.K., & Al-Kandari, A.J. (2014). The cultural-economic model and public relations in the Middle East: An examination of the Islamic banking system in Kuwait. *Public Relations Review, 40*(1), 33–41. https://doi.org/10.1016/j.pubrev.2013.11.003

Garcia, C. (2024). De-westernizing public relations: A comparative and global perspective on the influence of personal and patronage relationships across the world. *Catalan Journal of Communication and Cultural Studies,* 16(1), 83–99. https://doi.org/10.1386/cjcs_00096_1

Gidron, B., & Katz, H. (2024). Israel's civil society 2023 from protest to aid provision – A serving elite perspective. *Frontiers in Sociology, 9* https://doi.org/10.3389/fsoc.2024.1417687

Go-Globe (2024). Social media usage and trends in the Middle East. In www.go-globe.com/social-media-usage-in-middle-east-statistics/

Grunig J.E. (Ed.). (1992). *Excellence in Public Relations and Communication Management.* Hillsdale, NJ: Lawrence Erlbaum Associates.

Halff, G., & Gregory, A. (2013). Divided we stand: Defying hegemony in global public relations and practice? *Public Relations Review, 39*(5), 417–425. https://doi.org/10.1016/j.pubrev.2013.04.006

Hassan, A. (2023). Factors affecting the practice of public relations in the Middle East institutions. In R. El Khoury and N. Nasrallah (Eds.). *Emerging Trends and Innovation in Business and Finance. Contributions to Management Science*, pp. 639–651. Springer. https://doi.org/10.1007/978-981-99-6101-6_47

Holtzhausen, D.R. (2011). The need for a postmodern turn in global public relations. In N. Bardhan and C.K. Weaver (Eds.). *Public Relations in Global Contexts: Multi-paradigmatic Perspectives*, pp. 140–166. Routledge.

Jamil, S. (2022). Postulating the post-Arab spring dynamics of social media & digital journalism in the Middle East. *Digital Journalism, 10*(7), 1257–1261. https://doi.org/10.1080/21670811.2022.2040040

Katz, Y. (2019). Social media and new politics in the Middle East. *Journal of Social and Political Sciences,* 2(3). http://dx.doi.org/10.31014/aior.1991.02.03.120

Ki, E., Pasadeos, Y., & Ertem-Eray, T. (2021). The structure and evolution of global public relations: A citation and co-citation analysis 1983–2019. *Public Relations Review,* 47(1), 102012. https://doi.org/10.1016/j.pubrev.2021.102012

Ki, E., & Ye, L. (2017). An assessment of progress in research on global public relations from 2001 to 2014. *Public Relations Review, 43*(1), 235–245. https://doi.org/10.1016/j.pubrev.2016.12.005

Kirat, M. (2005). Public relations practice in the Arab World: A critical assessment. *Public Relations Review, 31*(3), 323–332. https://doi.org/10.1016/j.pubrev.2005.05.016

Kirat, M. (2015). Corporate social responsibility in the oil and gas industry in Qatar: Perceptions and practices. *Public Relations Review, 41*(4), 438–446. https://doi.org/10.1016/j.pubrev.2015.07.001

Lahav, T. (2016). The changing blogosphere and its impact on public relations practice and professional ethics: The Israeli case. *Public Relations Review, 42*(5), 929–931. https://doi.org/10.1016/j.pubrev.2016.08.006

Lahav, T., & Zimand-Sheiner, D. (2016). Public relations and the practice of paid content: Practical, theoretical propositions and ethical implications. *Public Relations Review, 42*(3), 395–401. https://doi.org/10.1016/j.pubrev.2016.02.003

Lee, S.W., Alsereidi, R.H., & Ben-Romdhane, S. (2023). Gender roles, gender bias, and cultural influences: Perceptions of male and female UAE public relations professionals. *Social Science, 12*(12), 673. https://doi.org/10.3390/socsci12120673

Leuppert, R., Allagui, I., & Klimmt, C. (2024). Social inequality and news media repertoires in seven MENA countries. *Global Media and Communication, 20*(3), 273–294. https://doi.org/10.1177/17427665241289262

Magen, C., & Lapid, E. (2016). Facing peace and war: Israel's Government Press Office, 1948–2014. *Public Relations Review, 42*(5), 776–786. https://doi.org/10.1016/j.pubrev.2016.08.004

Magen, C., & Lapid, E. (2018). Israel's military public diplomacy evolution: Historical and conceptual dimensions. *Public Relations Review, 44*(2), 287–298. https://doi.org/10.1016/j.pubrev.2017.11.003

Ni, W., & Sha, B.-L. (2018). *Intercultural public relations: Theories for managing relationships and conflicts with strategic publics*. Routledge.

Pal, M., & Dutta, M.J. (2008). Public relations in a global context: The relevance of critical modernism as a theoretical lens. *Journal of Public Relations Research, 20*(2), 159–179. https://doi.org/10.1080/1062726080 1894280

Pompper, D., & Adae, E.K. (2022). PR and sustainability across the African Continent: Using Afro-Centric philosophies to remember what's been 'forgotten or lost'. Paper Presented at the Annual Conference of the AEJMC.

Rechavi, A., Avidar, R., & Roth-Cohen, O. (2024). Geographical-institutional diversity and heterophily in academic research: A social network analysis of international collaboration, research communities and co-authorship in the public relations discipline. *Atlantic Journal of Communication, 33*(1), 71–93. https://doi.org/10.1080/15456870.2024.2371463

Selvik, K. (2013). Business and social responsibility in the Arab World: The Zakat vs. CSR models in Syria and Dubai. *Comparative Sociology, 12*, 95–123. https://doi.org/10.1163/15691330-12341254

Somma, E., & Rubino, A. (2016). Public-private participation in energy infrastructure in Middle East and North African countries: The role of institutions for renewable energy sources diffusion. *International Journal of Energy Economics and Policy, 6*(3), 621–629.

Sriramesh, K., Kim, Y., & Takasaki, M. (1999). Public relations in three Asian cultures: An analysis. *Journal of Public Relations Research, 11*(4), 271–292. https://doi.org/10.1207/s1532754xjprr1104_01

Sriramesh, K., & Vercic, D. (2003). A theoretical framework for global public relations research and practice. In K. Sriramesh and D. Vercic (Eds.). *The Global Public Relations Handbook*, pp. 1–19. Lawrence Erlbaum Associates.

Sriramesh, K., & Vercic, D. (2009). A theoretical framework for global public relations research and practice. In K. Sriramesh and D. Vercic (Eds.). *The Global Public Relations Handbook: Theory, Research and Practice* (2nd edition), pp. 3–21. New York, NY: Routledge. https://doi.org/10.4324/9780203889374

Sriramesh, K., & Vercic, D. (2019). *The global public relations handbook: Theory, research and practice*, (3rd edition). New York, NY: Routledge. https://doi.org/10.4324/9781315173290

Storie, L.K. (2015). Lost publics in public diplomacy: Antecedents for online relationship management. *Public Relations Review, 41*(2), 315–317. https://doi.org/10.1016/j.pubrev.2015.02.008

Swan, S. (2022). The Middle East. In *Routledge eBooks* (pp. 91–101). https://doi.org/10.4324/9781003155348-5

Sweetser, K.D., & Brown, C.W. (2008). Information subsidies and agenda-building during the Israel–Lebanon crisis. *Public Relations Review, 34*(4), 359–366. https://doi.org/10.1016/j.pubrev.2008.06.008

Sweetser, K.D., & Brown, C.W. (2010). An exploration of Iranian communication to multiple target audiences. *Public Relations Review, 36*(3), 238–248. https://doi.org/10.1016/j.pubrev.2010.03.005

Taylor, M. (2023). Reflections on the evolving theories of public relations. In C. Botan and E. Sommerfeldt (Eds.). *Public Relations Theory III – In the Age of Publics (ch. 30)*. Routledge.

Toledano, M., & Avidar, R. (2015). Public relations, ethics, and social media: A cross-national study of PR practitioners. *Public Relations Review, 42*(1), 161–169. https://doi.org/10.1016/j.pubrev.2015.11.012

Valentini, C., Kruckeberg, D., & Starck, K. (2016). The global society and its impact on public relations theorizing: Reflections on major macro trends. *Central European Journal of Communication, 9*(2), 229–246. https://doi.org/10.19195/1899-5101.9.2(17).6

Vercic, D., Grunig, L.A., & Grunig, J.E. (1996). Global and specific principles of public relations: Evidence from Slovenia. In H.M. Culbertson and N. Chen (Eds.). *International Public Relations: A Comparative Analysis*, pp. 31–65. Lawrence Erlbaum Associates.

Vollero, A., Yin, J., & Siano, A. (2022). Convergence or divergence? A comparative analysis of CSR communication by leading firms in Asia, Europe, and North America. *Public Relations Review, 48*(1). https://doi.org/10.1016/j.pubrev.2021.102142

White, C.L., & Alkandari, K. (2019). The influence of culture and infrastructure on CSR and country image: The case of Kuwait. *Public Relations Review, 45*(3), 101783. https://doi.org/10.1016/j.pubrev.2019.05.004

Zaharna, R.S. (2016). Beyond the individualism-collectivism divide to relationalism: Explicating cultural assumptions in the concept of "relationships". *Communication Theory, 26*(2), 190–211. https://doi.org/10.1111/comt.12058

Zayani, M. (2019). *Social movements in the digital age: Change and stasis in the Middle East.* European Institute of the Mediterranean (IEMed). In www.iemed.org/publication/social-movements-in-the-digital-age-change-and-stasis-in-the-middle-east/

Zhou et al. (2023). Exploring public relations research topics and inter-cluster dynamics through computational modeling (2010–2020): A study based on two SSCI journals. *Journal of Public Relations Research, 35*(3), 135–161. https://doi.org/10.1080/1062726X.2023.2180373

2 On organizational identity

Culturally grounded organizational identity formation

Ruth Avidar

Abstract

This chapter explores the complex process of organizational identity formation, emphasizing an organization's core values, beliefs, character, vision, and culture. While existing research in management and organizational studies often focuses on inter-organizational factors, it frequently overlooks the broader cultural context. Through the lens of public relations and using the GPRF framework, this chapter examines the role of cultural dynamics in organizational identity formation within the Israeli context, advocating for a holistic approach that integrates these unique cultural factors.

Organizational identity is a well-known and researched topic in the fields of management and organizational studies. One of its most familiar definitions from the 1980s is the features of an organization that are central, enduring, and distinct (Albert & Whetten, 1985), although since then the concept has undergone major changes, as will be further discussed.

Organizational identity and corporate identity

Organizational identity and corporate identity are two important, interconnected constructs that influence stakeholder trust and engagement with organizations. While organizational identity refers to the collective understanding and perception of an organization's values, beliefs, goals, and purpose by its internal stakeholders (Freeman & Koçak, 2023), corporate identity pertains to how the organization is perceived by its external stakeholders. For external stakeholders, such as customers, suppliers, investors, and regulators, corporate

DOI: 10.4324/9781003368366-2

identity is a key benchmark for assessing the organization's performance, societal value, and legitimacy (Freeman & Koçak, 2023). This encompasses elements such as visual identity (e.g., logo and design), communication strategies, and brand positioning (Lerpold et al., 2007; Sarasvuo, 2021), aligning it more closely with the concepts of "image" and "reputation".

Organizational identity is a widely studied concept in management and organizational studies, reflecting the core essence of an organization. It includes its fundamental values (Van Riel & Balmer, 1997), beliefs, and goals that define its purpose and character, as well as its mission statement (Sha, 2009), vision, culture, design, history, structure, behavior, strategy, and more. It represents the unique and enduring qualities that differentiate an organization from others. Organizational identity serves as the foundation that guides an organization's actions, decisions, and interactions. It provides a sense of direction for internal members and external stakeholders, offering clarity about what the organization represents and its unique contribution to the world (Ashforth et al., 2020; Xu, 2020). Research on organizational identity often emphasizes internal factors, including organizational culture, values, employees' perceptions of identity, their identification with the organization, and their sense of belonging and shared values (Liu et al., 2020; Ponting & Dillette, 2021). It is an interpretive framework that encapsulates the collective understanding of "who we are as an organization" (Ashforth et al., 2020; Whetten, 2006).

Research on corporate identity is primarily situated within the field of communication, focusing on how organizations present themselves to diverse audiences, including customers, employees, and investors. Corporate identity encompasses visual, verbal, and symbolic elements that convey a company's values, mission, and brand image. Key components include the logo, tagline, website design, and marketing materials, all integral to establishing a distinct brand identity (Lerpold et al., 2007; Sarasvuo, 2021). Corporate identity is a strategic asset that differentiates a company from its competitors and promotes a consistent brand image. Effectively managing this identity, through carefully designed symbols that reflect the organization's desired persona, is crucial for building trust, enhancing reputation, and nurturing positive stakeholder relationships (Dowling, & Otubanjo, 2011).

Corporate identity (external image and reputation) and organizational identity (internal perception and understanding) are argued to interact and influence stakeholder trust and engagement (Dowling &

Otubanjo, 2011). However, some studies adopt alternative frameworks to differentiate between these two constructs.

For example, Lerpold et al. (2007) argue that organizational identity has five dimensions that should reach a dynamic equilibrium to contribute to organizational performance. These dimensions that comprise "the organizational identity system" include the *professed identity* (used by management to define identity aspirations), the *projected identity* (projected through various media to strategic audiences), the *experienced identity* (members' beliefs of the organizational identity), the *manifested identity* (core traits of the organizational routines and achievements), and the *attributed identity* (the identity attributed to the organization by its audiences) (Lerpold, et.al., 2007).

The research on organizational identity has undergone a change in the last decades. In the past, it was argued that the manager of an organization is responsible for constructing a clear and consistent organizational identity. In the last decades, there is a growing understanding that organizational identity is not fixed but rather a dynamic, fluid (Gioia et al., 2000) and complex process that evolves over time and is influenced by shifting conditions in the organizational environment. It comprises various socially constructed meanings and practices, such as gender, nationality, and ethnicity (Curtin & Gaither, 2005; Madsen, 2016), shaped through a combination of factors such as the organization's history, leadership, culture, values, and interactions with stakeholders.

Nowadays, organizations actively engage in shaping and developing their identity to remain relevant, adapt to evolving contexts, and align with strategic objectives. This process often involves dialogue and collaboration with both internal and external stakeholders to co-create a shared understanding of organizational identity (Avidar, 2021; Gioia et al., 2010; He & Brown, 2013). As Theunissen (2014) notes, this co-creation "can only take place by means of a co-creational process" (pp. 613–614). Additionally, organizational identification plays a key role, reflecting the extent to which employees feel a sense of unity and belonging within their organization (Liu et al., 2020). Indeed, stakeholders use the stance of an organization on a certain issue as identity signals that enable them to decide whether the organization is an ally (Xu, 2020). In other words, the process of organizational identity formation is multifaceted, comprised of many internal and external powers, and therefore organizations are not completely free in choosing their identities.

Organizational and corporate identity influence both the internal and external aspects of an organization. Internally, a strong and coherent organizational identity can enhance employees' loyalty to the organization, aid in problem-solving and decision-making, foster internal trust, encourage inclusiveness and unity, and promote a stronger understanding of and connection to the organization's goals and mission statement (Freeman & Koçak, 2023). A recent study even found that "anthropomorphism," or attributing human qualities or behaviors to organizations, stimulates "interpersonal" emotions, actions, and accountability among organizational members. It also fosters social, relational, and personal identification with the organization while establishing a psychological contract (Liu et al., 2020).

Externally, a strong and coherent corporate identity can enhance trust among clients and customers, support reputation building and a positive image, influence financial performance, provide a competitive advantage, attract and retain talented employees, foster an innovative environment, and secure legitimacy by aligning with the rules, norms, and requirements of the external context (Albert & Whetten, 1985; Avidar, 2021; Bouchikhi & Kimberly, 2008; Konieczny et al., 2024).

Most research on organizational and corporate identity in the field of public relations focuses on single-identity organizations. However, in the fields of organizational studies and management, there is a growing emphasis on other forms of organizations such as "hybrid-identity" organizations that bring two different conceptualizations of "what is central, distinctive, and enduring about the organization" (Pratt & Foreman, 2000, p. 20) (e.g., a social business that embodies both a business-like and a societal identity); "multiple-identity" organizations that possess several distinct identities that coexist within the organizational structure. (Albert & Whetten, 1985; Foreman & Whetten, 2002) (e.g., a large university with distinct colleges or schools that each maintain their own identity in terms of academic culture, values, and priorities, yet are all part of the larger university system); and even a "fluid identity" organization, that "adopts a fluid and inherently dynamic identity to facilitate change in response to organizational demands" (Avidar, 2021, p. 6) (e.g., a Tech startup that pivots several times in its early stages [for example, from offering a consumer product to a B2B service model in response to market feedback and opportunities] before settling on a successful business model).

Public relations and the research of identity

There is a long history of research on public relations and identity (although not necessarily organizational/corporate identity or the process of organizational identity formation), as detailed and explained in the editorial by Sha (2018) for the special issue of the *Journal of public relations Research* on identity and public relations.

At first, identity in the field of public relations was explored at the level of the individual practitioner or practitioner groups, focusing on the identity of minority practitioners, and using various theoretical concepts based on race, ethnicity, gender, and sexual orientation (Sha, 2018). Other research on identity has explored the relationships and differences between organizational identity, reputation, and image (Huang-Horowitz, 2015; Theunissen, 2014). Identity was also explored through various theoretical lances, such as critical race theory (Logan, 2023), the cultural-economic model (Ciszek, 2017; Curtin & Gaither, 2005), relationship building (Xu, 2020), professional identity (Fawkes, 2015), corporate social responsibility (CSR) (Ozdora-Aksak & Atakan-Duman, 2015), co-creation, the dialogic theory (Theunissen, 2014), activism, intercultural public relations (Sha, 2006), and more.

However, research on organizational identity in the field of public relations often narrowed its focus to organizational type (e.g., nonprofit, corporate, and governmental) or organizational characteristics and inherent attributes (e.g., friendly, pleasant, open) (Men & Tsai, 2015). This is different from organizational identity, as the latter refers to features of an organization that represent the unique and enduring qualities that differentiate an organization from others (Xu, 2020).

It is important to recognize that research highlights the critical role public relations practitioners play in assisting organizations in constructing, reflecting, and communicating their identity and organizational culture to stakeholders (Bourland-Davis & Graham, 2017; Sha, 2009).

Public relations practitioners, as strategic communication experts, play a key role in helping organizations promote their identity through social media platforms, which have become vital channels for developing and projecting organizational identities. These platforms enable micro-interactions that enhance stakeholder engagement and communication (Czakon et al., 2024). Such interactions are critical in shaping an organization's digital identity, influenced by its communication with various stakeholders and defined by dimensions such as control, direction, values, and consciousness (Czakon et al., 2024). Moreover, social media content, including X (formerly Twitter) and Instagram posts, supports strategic communication by revealing the core values and beliefs of organizational members. This highlights the challenges of fragmented identity and its impact on internal coherence and external perceptions (Darics & Clifton, 2023; Watkins & Smith, 2022).

Cultural factors and organizational identity

Culture and cultural factors significantly influence the formation of organizational identity and an organization's ability to communicate this identity to its stakeholders. Public relations campaigns, in particular, are embedded with cultural meanings shaped by regulation, production (the meaning encoded by the organization), consumption (the reinterpretation of this meaning by consumers), and identity (Curtin & Gaither, 2007). Public relations practitioners act as intercultural mediators, offering organizations critical insights and facilitating effective communication across cultural boundaries. They possess motivation to communicate, knowledge of diverse cultures, and appropriate communication skills, which help them build relationships and navigate cultural differences (Tomohardjo et al., 2023).

Various scholars view the process of organizational identity formation as a co-creational process that can only take place if it involves both the organization and its publics (Theunissen, 2014). Nevertheless, despite the importance of cultural factors in organizational identity formation, most studies in the field of public relations fail to address the cultural context in which this process occurs. Additionally, much of this research is conducted within a U.S. or Western European context, predominantly reflecting Euro-American perspectives and theoretical frameworks. However, some studies have sought to highlight the differences between Euro-American perspectives and other cultural contexts, such as the Middle East, with its distinct cultural value orientations (Al-Kandari & Gaither, 2011; Creedon & Al-Khaja, 2019; Dhanesh & Avidar, 2023; Gaither & Al-Kandari, 2014; Kruckeberg, 1996; Watson, 2014).

I argue that although research on organizational identity formation in the field of public relations exists, it could be further developed and enriched by a more holistic approach that recognizes the importance of a wider array of cultural variables and their inherent impact on the process. This chapter will further elaborate on this issue by focusing on the Israeli cultural context.

The Israeli cultural context and the GPRF framework

To better understand the process of identity formation among Israeli organizations, we must look at the various cultural factors that characterize the Israeli system based on the GPRF framework. These factors collectively shape how organizations perceive and define themselves, how they communicate their identity to their stakeholders, and how they adapt to both local and global challenges and opportunities. An exploration of these cultural factors enables us to gain a deeper understanding of the diverse environments in which organizations operate, while allowing us to grasp the complex nuances and intricacies involved in applying concepts such as identity across different contexts.

In order not to explain the Israeli GPRF characteristics twice, this chapter will focus on the characteristics of the *Israeli political system, culture and religion, and activism,* while the next chapter (on reputation) will analyze the *economic system*, the *societal and organizational culture*, and the *media system*. However, it is important to keep in mind that although the five cultural features have been delineated individually, they are interconnected, thereby influencing and being influenced by one another.

Political system: The challenge of building a stable coalition

Israel is classified as a "free" country by Freedom House (2024), an organization that evaluates countries based on criteria such as the electoral system, political participation, government efficiency, and freedom of speech and belief. This classification indicates that Israel has a solid democratic system with political pluralism and active citizen involvement. This also signifies that Israel respects basic rights and freedoms and allows open political discourse and free expression of opinions.

The President of Israel is the head of state, but the position is mainly ceremonial, with limited executive powers. The Prime Minister, who is the head of government, holds supreme executive authority and is usually the leader of the party or coalition that has the most seats in the Knesset (the Israeli Parliament). The Prime Minister is responsible for forming a government and making key policy decisions. The state of Israel operates according to an electoral system of proportional representation, meaning the number of seats a party receives in the Knesset is proportional to the percentage of votes it receives in the national elections. The Knesset consists of 120 members who are elected for a four-year term (Galnoor & Blander, 2018).

Since the threshold for parties to enter the Knesset is relatively moderate (3.25% of the votes, or approximately 150,000 votes), the result is often a highly fragmented parliamentary landscape with many small parties representing a wide array of interests, faiths, ethnic origins, ideologies, and constituencies (Cohen, 2023; Hazan, 2020). For example, there are parties that represent secular Jews, religious Jews, Orthodox Jews, Arab citizens of Israel, economic interest groups, and immigrants from the former Soviet Union. Each group has distinct priorities and interests, making it challenging to form a government that can address the needs and demands of such a varied constituency. In addition, since its establishment, Israel has faced various challenges, including securing and defending its borders, the ongoing conflict with the Palestinians in the West Bank and Gaza, fragile relations between religion and the state (e.g., ongoing debates over the role of religion in public life and military conscription for Ultra-Orthodox men), differing opinions on economic and social policies, and more (Galnoor & Blander, 2018). Furthermore, the need to form coalitions among multiple parties, each with its own agenda and demands, complicates the process of government formation and often leads to unstable coalitions. It is argued that Israeli prime ministers often leverage electoral fragmentation to sustain their leadership, despite the inherent instability of the political landscape (Rosenthal, 2023).

In recent years, these challenges have been intensified by factors such as increasing polarization within Israeli society, internal crises (e.g., the government's attempts to weaken the Supreme Court's authority), external conflicts (e.g., the war with Hamas in Gaza, the Hezbollah in Lebanon, and the ongoing tensions with Iran and its proxies, including the Houthis from Yemen), and shifts in the global political landscape. These issues have contributed to repeated electoral cycles without decisive outcomes, further destabilizing the political situation and complicating the formation and maintenance of stable coalitions.

One of the key players in most Israeli coalitions is the Ultra-Orthodox Jewish parties, comprising approximately 1,175,000 people and representing 12.6% of the total population (Malach & Cahaner, 2021). These parties include Shas, which represents Sephardi and Mizrahi Haredi Judaism, and United Torah Judaism, which represents Ashkenazi Haredi Judaism.

These parties are valuable coalition partners, wielding significant political influence and playing a crucial role in coalition formation (Katz, 2024). Their cohesive voter base prioritizes religious issues, such as religious education, Sabbath observance, and control over personal status, ensuring consistent electoral support. By focusing on these issues, the Ultra-Orthodox parties can mobilize their constituencies effectively, securing a substantial number of seats in the Knesset. This influence allows them to leverage concessions and shape policy-making, as seen in their demands for military service exemptions for Ultra-Orthodox males (Katz, 2024). The fragmented nature of Israeli politics often requires forming coalitions with Ultra-Orthodox parties, enabling them to influence policy priorities and advance their goals. Their political power shifts with the political context and election cycles, also shaping organizational identity, as will be further explored.

Culture and religion: A tapestry of diverse cultures, religions, and ethnic groups

Israel's society is incredibly diverse, characterized by a rich tapestry of cultural, religious, and ethnic groups, along with unique societal factors shaped by historical, geographical, and political influences (Rebhun, 2023). Israel is home to nearly 10 million residents, of whom 73% are Jewish, 20% are Arab (Muslim, Christian, or Druze), and 6% are classified as "others" (Central Bureau of Statistics, 2022).

The Israeli Arab population is the largest minority in Israel, including Muslims, Christians, and Druze, each with their own cultural and religious identities. They share language and cultural ties with the broader Arab world while also engaging with the Israeli state and society. Israel upholds democratic principles that guarantee freedom of religion and conscience to all its citizens. The state recognizes and supports all religious communities and provides them with autonomy in the management of their religious affairs. Each religious community has its own religious courts that oversee matters such as marriage, divorce, and other issues of personal status within their communities (Westreich & Westreich, 2023).

While Judaism is the majority religion, there is significant variation within it, from the Ultra-Orthodox (Haredi) and Orthodox communities to Conservative, Reform, and secular Jews who may identify culturally rather than religiously (Y.J. Katz, 2018). The Jewish population of Israel includes immigrants from over 100 countries across all continents, each contributing unique traditions, languages, cultural practices, and interests. This diversity shapes Israel's complex and dynamic social fabric. The interplay of these elements fosters rich cultural diversity while also fueling ongoing and intensifying social and political debates (Ben-Rafael, 2007).

Most Israeli citizens define themselves as "secular" (43.5%), followed by "traditional to varying degrees" (27.4%), "religious" (16.7%), and "Haredi" (8.0%) (Central Bureau of Statistics, 2022). The secular population, a significant part of Israeli society, consists of people who do not adhere to certain customs or religious affiliation (Y.J. Katz, 2018). Secular Israelis often give priority to secular values, democratic principles, and cultural identity over religious observance. Many of them advocate liberal values such as individual freedoms, equality, and social justice. Liberal voices can be found across the religious-secular spectrum, with differing opinions on issues such as civil rights, gender equality, and peace processes.

Among the Jewish secular community, there is a large group of citizens of the former Soviet Union who immigrated (made *Aliya*h) to Israel in the period of 1989–2002. Many of them define themselves as "secular" (Shaps, 2016), and often navigate multifaceted identities, blending Soviet, Jewish, Israeli, and Western elements (Leybenson et al., 2022). They mostly speak Hebrew, serve in the Israeli Defense Forces (IDF), and support the strengthening of secular symbols, the introduction of civil marriages, and the existence of public transportation and the opening of places of recreation on Shabbat, the Jewish Sabbath, observed on Saturday (Ilani, 2006).

Since there is no separation between religion and state, Judaism plays a significant role in Israeli identity and the legal framework, leading to ongoing debates, crises, and discussions about the role of religion in public life. Issues such as religious pluralism, the recognition of non-Orthodox streams of Judaism, and the influence of religious institutions on matters of personal status often spark public and political discourse and debates. These debates stem from differing viewpoints within Israeli society regarding the balance between Jewish tradition and democratic values (Rebhun, 2023). In recent years, it has been argued that the desire to maintain a balance between the democratic and Jewish aspects of the state has declined. Outside of the secular public, there is a growing preference within the Jewish majority for emphasizing the Jewish aspect over the democratic one (The Israel Democracy Institute, 2022). Indeed, religious issues hold a significant place in Israeli society, given the state's identity as a Jewish state and the lack of separation between religion and state. Topics such as religious freedom, access to holy sites, and the role of religious institutions in public life resonate deeply with many Israelis. Ultra-Orthodox parties position themselves as authorities on these matters, garnering support from those who prioritize religious values and traditions (Rebhun, 2023).

Activism: Engaging in public discourse and advocating for change

Israel's foundation, shaped by the convergence of immigrants from diverse cultural backgrounds and immediate security challenges, fostered a strong culture of activism and advocacy among its citizens (Ben-Rafael, 2007). This activism is reflected in the dynamic political landscape, where various groups advocate for their interests, and in vibrant social movements influenced by a citizenship regime that blends liberal, republican, and ethnonational principles, shaping their mobilization and practices (Sparr, 2022). The activism scene reflects the country's democratic values and its citizens' willingness to engage in public discourse and advocate for change.

The diversity of Israeli society is evident in the broad spectrum of causes and movements that activism addresses, spanning peace and security, social and economic justice, environmental issues, religious pluralism, and freedom (Rebhun, 2023), as well as LGBTQ+ and minority rights (Ben-David & Rubel-Lifschitz, 2017).

In 2023–2025, significant activism emerged in response to the government's attempt to weaken the Supreme Court, followed by widespread mobilization during the Israel-Hamas war and efforts to secure the release of Israeli hostages abducted by Hamas. Regarding the former, the government's proposed judicial overhaul sought to limit the Court's authority to review and overturn legislation, thereby increasing executive control over the judiciary. This proposal sparked widespread public outcry, culminating in one of the largest protest movements in Israel's history and underscoring the strong commitment of many Israelis to safeguarding the rule of law and maintaining checks and balances within the democratic system (Lubell, 2023).

As for the war with Hamas, many organizations that had protested against the judicial overhaul shifted their focus on October 7, 2023, to providing aid. This transition highlighted the emergence of a "Serving Elite," a group reshaping societal power dynamics by combining activism with aid efforts (Gidron & Katz, 2024). The complexity of Israeli activism is further illustrated by female activists within Israel's Islamic movement, who navigate identities that balance integration and seclusion while adopting humanistic approaches to bridge religious and civic identities (Alinat-Abed, 2024). These diverse forms of activism highlight Israel's multifaceted social, political, and cultural landscape, where various groups engage in efforts to address evolving challenges and shape the country's future.

Building on an exploration of the cultural factors shaping Israeli society, this chapter presents a holistic framework for understanding organizational identity and culture, grounded in the GPRF model.

A holistic approach to organizational identity formation

Organizational identity represents the essence of an organization, encompassing its core values, beliefs, mission, vision, culture, and design. It is shaped by the interaction between organizational characteristics and the cultural context, as defined by the GPRF framework. This chapter argues that "culture," in its broader sense, not only *affects* the process of identity formation but is *integral to its very fabric*, deeply influencing the process itself. Accordingly, this chapter proposes a version of organizational identity formation that incorporates these cultural nuances, offering a more holistic and culturally appropriate framework. Additionally, a relevant case study is presented and discussed to illustrate this approach.

Culturally grounded organizational identity formation

The Culturally Grounded Organizational Identity Formation (CGOIF) framework represents a dynamic process through which organizations develop and articulate their identity by integrating the diverse cultural landscapes that shape their environment into their core essence. This process does not occur in isolation but involves continuous negotiation and adaptation between the organization's internal and external cultural environments. According to this framework, organizational identity formation operates within a dynamic ecosystem influenced by ongoing interactions with various cultural, economic, and sociopolitical elements. While this chapter focuses on the Israeli context, the CGOIF framework is designed to be applicable across diverse cultural contexts worldwide.

The four components of the CGOIF framework:

1 *Cultural Integration*
Cultural integration involves embedding core cultural values into an organization's identity. These values are shaped by the national character, historical experiences, and collective memory. In the Israeli context, they include resilience, adaptability, religious and cultural heritage, courage, mutual responsibility and solidarity (*Kol Israel Arevim Zeh Lazeh*—"All of Israel are responsible for one another"), the importance of family and home, and a strong sense of community and unity (*Achdut* in Hebrew), which have been increasingly challenged in recent years (Sassoni-Bar Lev & Avidar, 2023a; 2023b).
2 *Political and Economic Responsiveness*
Political and economic responsiveness reflects an organization's ability to adapt its identity to changing political and economic conditions. In Israel's complex political, security, and economic landscape, this adaptability is evident in flexibility, creativity, compliance with emergency situations, technological innovation and leadership, and balancing political awareness with economic responsiveness.
3 *Diversity, equity, and Inclusion*
Diversity, equity, and inclusion encompass the acknowledgment of religious and ethnic diversity alongside a commitment to cultural sensitivity and inclusivity, both within the organization and in society. This component emphasizes integrating these principles into the process of an organization's identity formation. In Israel, this involves recognizing and respecting the diverse ethnicities, religions, and cultures within the workforce (including both management and employees) as well as in the broader society. Key expressions include societal inclusiveness, religious sensitivity and freedom, tolerance, tradition, pluralism, unity, integration, and multiculturalism.

4 *Societal Engagement*
   Societal engagement reflects how an organization aligns and co-creates its identity while engaging with its stakeholders and addressing the concerns, values, and aspirations of the society it serves. In the Israeli context, this includes fostering harmony and coexistence between secular and religious groups, as well as between Israeli and Arab citizens. For example, in 2021, as violence between Jews and Arabs escalated in mixed cities in Israel, hospital staff (including medical, nursing, and administrative teams) highlighted the value of "unity" embodied in the hospitals' identity, where Jews and Arabs work together, by initiating a campaign featuring employees of different faiths under messages of peace, coexistence, unity, and solidarity (Ma'anit, 2021).

To summarize, the suggested framework positions culture as a fundamental element intricately linked to the process of organizational identity formation and co-creation, rather than merely an external influence. Culture shapes how organizations perceive themselves, their mission, and their values, embedding the cultural context into identity formation. Simultaneously, organizational identity reflects internally on workplace relationships and externally through corporate identity, creating a reciprocal relationship in which culture shapes and is shaped by organizational identity. For Israeli organizations, this involves navigating a complex landscape of security concerns, uncertainty, historical legacies, and political, religious, and social dynamics. By advocating for a culturally grounded, holistic approach, the framework highlights the integration of a country's unique cultural dimensions into identity formation. This approach provides a nuanced understanding of how organizations navigate and contribute to their societal and cultural environments, resulting in identities that are authentic, adaptive, and deeply connected to the communities they serve.

The following sample campaign illustrates the framework and demonstrates how a country's cultural dimensions are incorporated into the process of organizational identity formation.

Case study: Tiv Ta'am's identity transformation – Navigating political-religious challenges to define freedom of choice

Tiv Ta'am Chains Ltd., operating under the brand "Tiv Ta'am" (www.tivtaam.co.il), is an Israeli food marketing chain established in

1990. The chain specializes in the production, import, and marketing of a wide range of food products. Notably, Tiv Ta'am sells mainly nonkosher food, and most of its branches remain open seven days a week, including Shabbat and holidays, except for Yom Kippur.

In the early 2000s, the chain underwent various organizational changes, both in its holdings and product offerings, and appeared to struggle with defining its core essence and primary attributes. For example, in a series of campaigns, the chain utilized chefs and public opinion leaders to highlight the *quality and uniqueness* of its products. Later, it featured a Ukraine-oriented celebrity in a campaign emphasizing the chain's *fair prices and excellent customer experience* (Allmarketing, n.d.).

The political turbulence of 2018, shaped by the interplay between the Israeli political system, religion-state dynamics, and heightened activism, compelled the company to explicitly define its identity and reassess its fundamental values and beliefs. To better understand this transformation, it is necessary to examine its historical roots.

Since 2013, Israel's complex political system and the interplay between religion and state have fueled a series of conflicts between the Knesset and the Supreme Court. This confrontation peaked in 2013 when the Supreme Court compelled the Tel Aviv municipality to either close all businesses on Shabbat, as required by its municipal law, or amend the law (Meganzi, 2013). In response, the municipality revised the law, and in 2017, the Supreme Court approved the new legislation, allowing supermarkets in Tel Aviv to operate on Shabbat. However, due to political-coalitional considerations, the Interior Ministers from 2013 to 2017 refused to sign and implement the law, prompting the Supreme Court to intervene and approve it independently (Fridson, 2017). In response, the Knesset passed the "Supermarket Law," which bypassed the Supreme Court's decision by stipulating that a local authority may not amend municipal legislation to permit commercial activity on Shabbat within its jurisdiction without the interior minister's approval (Nachshoni, 2019). At the time, this position was held by an Ultra-Orthodox politician from the Shas party. The practical implication of this law was that most supermarkets, including Tiv Ta'am's main branch in Tel Aviv, were prohibited from operating on Shabbat, traditionally a popular shopping day for secular customers.

An exploration of news articles suggests that the "Supermarket Law" served as a catalyst for a significant and a well-defined process of organizational identity formation undertaken by Tiv Ta'am (N12

News, 2019). It seems that the political and cultural upheaval caused by the legislation prompted the chain's management to recognize the need to refine and focus their unique identity and core values. This aligns with the *political and economic responsiveness* component of the CGOIF framework, which reflects an organization's ability to adapt its identity to evolving political and economic conditions. Rather than focusing solely on "fair prices" or "quality products" (though still important), Tiv Ta'am adopted principles of pluralism, cultural diversity, and "freedom to choose"—values tied to the *diversity, equity, and inclusion* component of the CGOIF framework, which also became the chain's slogan (Raz-Haimovich, 2018). In essence, Tiv Ta'am's organizational identity formation both embraced and reflected the concerns, values, and aspirations of Israeli society.

Moreover, the chain aligned its identity with the concerns, values, and aspirations of society by taking a definitive stance in the political and cultural debate. It launched an activist, ideological campaign under the slogan, "It's Only a Supermarket" (Benjamin, 2019). This campaign, which included an online petition, connected the "Supermarket Law" to broader religious and anti-liberal policies. These included the lack of public transportation on Shabbat, restrictions on selling nonkosher food in public hospitals, the prevention of ultra-Orthodox military recruitment, the exclusion of women from the public sphere, and discrimination against the LGBTQ+ community (YouTube, 2019). This action aligned with the *societal engagement* component of the framework, emphasizing the importance of addressing challenges through organizational activism, participation, and outreach.

It seems that this process of organizational identity formation also led the chain to openly acknowledge that many of its customers were immigrants from the former Soviet Union who shop on Shabbat and do not eat kosher food. Furthermore, the chain positioned itself as a voice for the secular population, empowering and encouraging its customers to live according to their preferences and lifestyle. It emphasized values such as pluralism, multiculturalism, and freedom of choice. As the company's CEO explained: "Tiv Ta'am represents liberal Israeliism, rooted in Israel's identity as a multicultural state in the spirit of the Declaration of Independence. It reflects an Israeliness that allows each and every one of us to choose how we want to live our lives according to our faith and preferences. Standing at the forefront of the struggle for freedom of choice, it reminds us that we all have the freedom to act and live as we wish, even on weekends" (A. Katz, 2018, translated from Hebrew).

The campaign was launched across both digital and traditional platforms, garnering significant media and public attention while provoking strong reactions from Ultra-Orthodox political parties. The Shas party even petitioned the Supreme Court, demanding the removal of the campaign video on the grounds that it constituted political propaganda during the election period; however, the Supreme Court rejected the request (Hazani, 2019).

This campaign exemplifies the dynamic process through which organizations develop and articulate their identity by integrating diverse cultural characteristics into their identity formation. As demonstrated, organizational identity formation is not an isolated process but involves continuous negotiation and adjustment between the organization's perceptions, values, and beliefs and the cultural context in which it operates.

Questions for further discussion

1. How is the process of organizational identity formation carried out in nondemocratic regimes? How do the political characteristics of such regimes influence an organization's ability to define its core values?
2. How can organizational identity be designed in a multinational organization operating in multiple countries? Should the organization maintain a unified identity, or can it develop multiple identities tailored to different cultural contexts?
3. Can you provide a real-world example of an organizational identity formation process in which the organization effectively reflects and addresses the concerns, values, and aspirations of the society it serves?
4. Can you think of additional components that could be included in the Culturally Grounded Organizational Identity Formation framework?

References

Albert, S., & Whetten, D.A. (1985). Organizational identity. *Research in Organizational Behavior, 7*, 263–295.

Alinat-Abed, S. (2024). Navigating in insecure territory: Attitudes among Islamic movement female activists toward the Israeli authorities and culture. *Politics and Religion Journal, 18*(1). https://doi.org/10.54561/prj1801187a

Al-Kandari, A., & Gaither, T.K. (2011). Arabs, the west and public relations: A critical/cultural study of Arab cultural values, *Public Relations Review, 37*(3), 266–273. https://doi.org/10.1016/j.pubrev.2011.04.002

Allmarketing (n.d.). Nicole Raidman will lead a campaign for Tiv Ta'am. www.allmarketing.co.il/%D7%A0%D7%99%D7%A7%D7%95%D7%9C-%D7%A8%D7%90%D7%99%D7%93%D7%9E%D7%9F-%D7%AA%D7%95%D7%91%D7%99%D7%9C-%D7%A7%D7%9E%D7%A4%D7%99%D7%99%D7%9F-%D7%A9%D7%9C-%D7%98%D7%99%D7%91-%D7%98%D7%A2%D7%9D/ [Hebrew].

Ashforth, B.E., Schinoff, B.S., & Brickson, S.L. (2020). "My company is friendly," "Mine a rebel": Anthropomorphism and shifting organizational identity from "what" to "who". *Academy of Management Review, 45*(1). https://doi.org/10.5465/amr.2016.0496

Avidar, R. (2021). The challenge of building a favorable reputation for social businesses. *Social Business, 11*(1–2), 80–99. https://doi.org/10.1362/204440821X16206324311178

Ben-David, Y., & Rubel-Lifschitz, T. (2017). Practice the change you want to see in the world: Transformative practices of social movements in Israel. *Peace and Conflict: Journal of Peace Psychology, 24*(1), 10–18. https://psycnet.apa.org/doi/10.1037/pac0000268

Benjamin, M. (2019, September 16). Just a supermarket, but what a commotion: Tiv Ta'am has become the talk of the town. *ICE*. www.ice.co.il/advertising-marketing/news/article/768369 [Hebrew].

Ben-Rafael, E. (2007). Mizrahi and Russian challenges to Israel's dominant culture: Divergences and convergences. *Israel Studies, 12*(3), 68–91. https://doi.org/10.2979/ISR.2007.12.3.68

Bouchikhi, H. & Kimberly, J.R. (2008). *The Soul of the Corporation: How to Manage the Identity of Your Company*. Wharton School Publishing.

Bourland-Davis, P.G. & Graham, B.L. (2017). Examining public relations' role in shaping organizational culture, with implications for PR, HR, and CSR/Sustainability. In D. Pompper (Ed.). *Corporate Social Responsibility, Sustainability, and Ethical Public Relations* (*The Changing Context of Managing People*, pp. 199–219. Emerald Publishing. https://doi.org/10.1108/978-1-78714-585-620181008

Central Bureau of Statistics. (2022). *2022 census data*. https://census.cbs.gov.il/he

Ciszek, E. (2017). Public relations, activism and identity: A cultural-economic examination of contemporary LGBT activism, *Public Relations Review, 43*(4), 809–816. https://doi.org/10.1016/j.pubrev.2017.01.005

Cohen, E. (2023). Political instability in Israel over the last decades – Causes and consequences. *Cogent Social Sciences, 10*(1). https://doi.org/10.1080/23311886.2023.2293316

Creedon, P., & Al-Khaja, M. (2019). An overview of Middle East public relations practice, education, and research from isolation to globalization, *Journal of Public Relations Research, 31*(3–4), 84–96. https://doi.org/10.1080/1062726X.2019.1682324

Curtin, P.A., & Gaither, T.K. (2005). Privileging identity, difference, and power: The circuit of culture as a basis for public relations practice. *Journal of Public Relations Research, 17*, 91–115. https://doi.org/10.1207/s1532754xjprr1702_3

Curtin, P.A., & Gaither, T.K. (2007). *International public relations: Negotiating culture, identity, and power*. Sage. https://doi.org/10.4135/9781452224817

Czakon, W., Mania, K., Jedynak, M., Kuźniarska, A., Choiński, M., & Dabić, M. (2024). Who are we? Analyzing the digital identities of organizations through the lens of micro-interactions on social media. *Technological Forecasting and Social Change, 198*, 123012. https://doi.org/10.1016/j.techfore.2023.123012

Darics, E., & Clifton, J. (2023). Tracking the identity of the organisation via Twitter: Metadiscourse analysis. In *Organisation, Communication and Language. New Perspectives in Organizational Communication*. Palgrave Macmillan. https://doi.org/10.1007/978-3-031-30199-5_6

Dhanesh, G.S., & Avidar, R. (2023). Culture and dialog theory in public relations: The Middle Eastern context. In E. Sommerfeldt and C. Botan (Eds.). *Public Relations Theory* (3rd edition), pp. 321–337. Routledge. ISBN: 9780367683313.

Dowling, G.R., & Otubanjo, T. (2011). Corporate and organizational identity: Two sides of the same coin. *AMS Review, 1*(3), 171–182. https://doi.org/10.1007/s13162-011-0022-1

Fawkes, O. (2015). Performance and persona: Goffman and Jung's approaches to professional identity applied to public relations, *Public Relations Review, 41*(5), 675–680. https://doi.org/10.1016/j.pubrev.2014.02.011

Foreman, P., & Whetten, D.A. (2002). Member's identification with multiple-identity organizations. *Organization Science, 13*(6), 618–635. https://doi.org/10.1287/orsc.13.6.618.493

Freedom House. (2024). *Expanding freedom and democracy*. https://freedomhouse.org/countries/freedom-world/scores

Freeman, A., & Koçak, Ö. (2023). Designing inclusive organizational identities. *Journal of Organization Design, 12*, 177–193. https://doi.org/10.1007/s41469-023-00150-0

Fridson, Y. (2017, October 26). Supreme Court: Supermarkets in Tel Aviv will continue operating on Shabbat. *Ynet*. www.ynet.co.il/articles/0,7340,L-5033973,00.html [Hebrew].

Gaither, T.K., & Al-Kandari, A.J. (2014). The cultural-economic model and public relations in the Middle East: An examination of the Islamic banking system in Kuwait, *Public Relations Review, 40*(1), 33–41. https://doi.org/10.1016/j.pubrev.2013.11.003

Galnoor, I., & Blander, D. (2018). *The handbook of Israel's political system*. Cambridge University Press. https://doi.org/10.1017/9781316160978

Gidron, B., & Katz, H. (2024). Israel's civil society 2023 from protest to aid provision – A serving elite perspective. *Frontiers in Sociology, 9*. https://doi.org/10.3389/fsoc.2024.1417687

Gioia, D.A., Price, K.N., Hamilton, A.L., & Thomas, J.B. (2010). Forging an identity: An insider-outsider study of processes involved in the formation of organizational identity. *Administrative Science Quarterly, 55*, 1–46. https://doi.org/10.2189/asqu.2010.55.1.1

Gioia, D.A., Schultz, M., & Corley, K.G. (2000). Organizational identity, image, and adaptive instability. *Academy of Management Review, 25*(1), 63–81. https://doi.org/10.2307/259263

Hazan, R.Y. (2020). Parties and the party system of Israel. In Reuven Y. Hazan and others (Eds.). *The Oxford Handbook of Israeli Politics and Society*, pp. 350–366. Oxford Academic. https://doi.org/10.1093/oxfordhb/9780190675585.013.21_update_001

Hazani, G. (2019, September 17). Shas petitioned the Election Committee against a Tiv Ta'am advertisement – Justice Melcer rejected the petition. *Calcalist*. [Hebrew]. www.calcalist.co.il/local/articles/0,7340,L-3770549,00.html

He, H., & Brown, A.D. (2013). Organizational identity and organizational identification: A review of the literature and suggestions for future research. *Group & Organization Management, 38*, 3–35. https://doi.org/10.1177/1059601112473815

Huang-Horowitz, N.C. (2015). Public relations in the small business environment: Creating identity and building reputation. *Public Relations Review, 41*, 345–353. https://doi.org/10.1016/j.pubrev.2014.10.018

Ilani, O. (2006). *Religion, society, and state in Israel*. The Center for Educational Technology.

Katz, A. (2018, March 7). While the fight to close shops on Shabbat goes on: A new campaign for Tiv Ta'am. *ICE*. [Hebrew] www.ice.co.il/advertising-marketing/news/article/737535

Katz, Y. (2024). Identity politics and religious in modern society. *International Journal of Scientific and Management Research, 7*(9), 49–60. http://doi.org/10.37502/IJSMR.2024.7904

Katz, Y.J. (2018). Religious and heritage education in Israel in an era of secularism. *Education Sciences, 8*(4), 176. https://doi.org/10.3390/educsci8040176

Konieczny, G.J., Kolisnichenko, P., Górska, M., & Gorski, T. (2024). Identity of an enterprise as a distinct value in a culture of high tolerance for uncertainty. *Economics, Finance and Management Review, 3*(19), 100–109. https://doi.org/10.36690/2674-5208-2024-3-100-109

Kruckeberg, D. (1996). A global perspective on public relations ethics: The Middle East. *Public Relations Review, 22*(2), 181–189. https://doi.org/10.1016/S0363-8111(96)90006-5

Lerpold, L., Ravasi, D., Ven Rekom, J., & Soenen, G. (2007). *Organizational identity in practice.* Routledge. ISBN: 9780415398404

Leybenson, M., Gutman, M., & Yemini, M. (2022). Crossing the borders: Dynamic identity variations of former Israeli Russian-speaking migrants of the 1.5 generation. *Journal of Borderlands Studies, 39*(3), 495–512. https://doi.org/10.1080/08865655.2022.2151033

Liu, H., Bracht, E., Zhang, X., Bradley, B., & Van Dick, R. (2020). Creativity in non-routine jobs: The role of transformational leadership and organizational identification. *Creativity and Innovation Management.* https://doi.org/10.1111/caim.12419

Logan, N. (2023). Critical race theory, identity, and public relations. In E. Sommerfeldt and C. Botan (Eds.). *Public Relations Theory III*, pp. 285–302. Routledge. ISBN: 9780367683313.

Lubell, M. (2023, September 12). Protests grip Israel ahead of historic Supreme Court session. *Reuters.* www.reuters.com/world/middle-east/israel-edge-ahead-supreme-court-session-judicial-overhaul-2023-09-11/

Ma'anit, H. (2021, May 13). There is also hope: Reconciliation initiatives and solidarity events between Jews and Arabs. *Globes.* www.globes.co.il/news/article.aspx?did=1001371001 [Hebrew].

Madsen, V.T. (2016). Constructing organizational identity on internal social media: A case study of coworker communication in Jyske Bank. *International Journal of Business Communication, 53*(2), 200–223. https://doi.org/10.1177/2329488415627272

Malach, G., & Cahaner, L. (2021). *Statistical report on ultra-orthodox society in Israel.* The Israel Democracy Institute. https://en.idi.org.il/haredi/2020/?chapter=34272

Meganzi, A. (2013, June 25). Supreme Court: Tel Aviv municipality to act on closing businesses on Shabbat. *Ynet.* [Hebrew]. www.ynet.co.il/articles/0,7340,L-4396897,00.html

Men, L.R., & Tsai, W.H.S. (2015). Infusing social media with humanity: Corporate character, public engagement, and relational outcomes. *Public Relations Review, 41*(3), 395–403. https://doi.org/10.1016/j.pubrev.2015.02.005

N12 News (2019, September 11). The campaign of "Tiv Taam" against religious coercion. [Hebrew]. www.mako.co.il/news-channel2/Economy-Newcast-2019_Q3/Article-f618fbf97712d61026.htm.

Nachshoni, K. (2019, April 1). The Supermarkets Law: The Government bypassed the Supreme Court. *Ynet.* [Hebrew] www.ynet.co.il/articles/0,7340,L-5458823,00.html.

Ozdora-Aksak, E., & Atakan-Duman, S. (2015). The online presence of Turkish banks: Communicating the softer side of corporate identity. *Public Relations Review, 41*(1), 119–128. https://doi.org/10.1016/j.pubrev.2014.10.004

Ponting, S.S., & Dillette, A. (2021). (Dis)connected organizational identity of multinational hotel corporations: Employee insights from a Mexican luxury hotel property, *Tourism and Hospitality Research, 21*(1), 86–98. https://doi.org/10.1177/1467358420970633

Pratt, M.G., & Foreman, P.O. (2000). Classifying managerial responses to multiple organizational identities. *Academy of Management Review, 25*, 18–42. https://doi.org/10.5465/amr.2000.2791601

Raz-Haimovich, M. (March 7, 2018). Tiv Ta'am will try to keep stores open on Shabbat in a new campaign. *Globes*. [Hebrew]. www.globes.co.il/news/article.aspx?did=1001226691.

Rebhun, U. (2023). Jewish diversity in Israel. *European Judaism, 56*(2), 88–111. https://doi.org/10.3167/ej.2023.560209

Rosenthal, M. (2023). *Israel's electoral system and political instability. Routledge handbook on elections in the Middle East and North Africa*. Routledge. ISBN: 9781003185628.

Sarasvuo, S. (2021). Are we one, or are we many? Diversity in organizational identities versus corporate identities. *Journal of Product & Brand Management, 30*(6), 788–805. https://doi.org/10.1108/JPBM-03-2020-2827

Sassoni-Bar Lev, O., & Avidar, R. (2023a). 'God forbid we'd be infected': Framing and counter-framing of the 'Corona Cruise Ship' in Israeli media. *The Journal of International Communication, 29*(2), 213–233. https://doi.org/10.1080/13216597.2023.2203687

Sassoni-Bar Lev, O., & Avidar, R. (2023b). 'And parents shall come again to their own border': Belonging and solidarity in the face of exclusion and anxiety in the media coverage of the Corona Ship. In H. Hazaz-Berger, G. Yair and T. Gamliel (Eds.). *Urgent Ethnography: Aspects and Challenges in the Corona Plague*. University of Bar-Ilan. [Hebrew]. ISBN: 9789652266507.

Sha, B.L. (2006). Cultural identity in the segmentation of publics: An emerging theory of intercultural public relations. *Journal of Public Relations Research, 18*(1), 45–65. https://doi.org/10.1207/s1532754xjprr1801_3

Sha, B.L. (2009). Exploring the connection between organizational identity and public relations behaviors: How symmetry trumps conservation in engendering organizational identification. *Journal of Public Relations Research, 21*(3), 295–317. https://doi.org/10.1080/10627260802640765

Sha, B.L. (2018). Editor's essay: Identity and/in/of public relations. *Journal of Public Relations Research, 30*(4), 129–133. https://doi.org/10.1080/1062726X.2018.1534339

Shaps, M. (2016). Selected data on the population of Israeli immigrants from the former Soviet Union on the occasion of twenty-five years to the wave of

Aliyah. *Hed Haulpan Hahadash*, 105 [Hebrew]. https://meyda.education.gov.il/files/AdultEducation/hed_haulpan/hed_105_marina_sheps.pdf

Sparr, K. (2022). *Israeli social movements. The Wiley*-Blackwell encyclopedia of social and political movements, 1–4. Wiley. Online ISBN: 9780470674871.

The Israel Democracy Institute (2022). *Yearbook of the ultra-orthodox society*. www.idi.org.il/haredi/2022/?chapter=46893

Theunissen, P. (2014). Co-creating corporate identity through dialogue: A pilot study. *Public Relations Review, 40*(3), 612–614. https://doi.org/10.1016/j.pubrev.2014.02.026

Tomohardjo, I., Ahmad, M., & Amrullah, H.F. (2023). Bridging cultures: Intercultural communication in public relations for Jakarta practitioners. *Profetik: Jurnal Komunikasi, 16*(2), 217–235. https://doi.org/10.14421/pjk.v16i2.2598

Van Riel, C.B.M., & Balmer, J.M.T. (1997). Corporate identity: The concept, its measurement and management. *European Journal of Marketing, 31*(5), 340–55. https://doi.org/10.1108/eb060635

Watkins, B., & Smith, S.A. (2022). I want to work there: How public relations agencies communicate organizational culture and identity on Instagram. *Journal of Communication Management, 26*(1), 58–83. https://doi.org/10.1108/JCOM-01-2021-0005

Watson, T. (2014). *Middle Eastern and African perspectives on the development of public relations: Other voices.* Palgrave Macmillan. ISBN: 9781137404275.

Westreich, E., & Westreich, A. (2023). Rabbinical court decisions and their impact on Jewish society. In *Brill | Nijhoff eBooks*, pp. 153–174. https://doi.org/10.1163/9789004446816_008

Whetten, D.A. (2006). Albert and Whetten revisited: Strengthening the concept of organizational identity. *Journal of management inquiry, 15*(3), 219–234. https://doi.org/10.1177/1056492606291200

Xu, S. (2020). Issues, identity salience, and individual sense of connection to organizations: an identity-based approach. *Journal of Public Relations Research, 32*(3–4), 120–139. https://doi.org/10.1080/1062726X.2020.1802731

YouTube (2019). *It's only a supermarket.* [Hebrew]. www.youtube.com/watch?v=lpepHrhIUwQ

3 On organizational reputation

A culturally embedded organizational reputation model

Ruth Avidar

Abstract

Organizational reputation reflects the collective perceptions and judgments of an organization's external and internal stakeholders, including employees, customers, and the media. It is influenced by past actions, behaviors, and performance in areas such as ethics, sustainability, quality, reliability, and financial stability. As a valuable intangible asset, reputation plays a critical role in an organization's success. This chapter examines the relationship between organizational reputation and cultural factors in the Israeli context through the GPRF framework. It highlights how Israeli organizations build and manage their reputation by aligning with cultural values such as mutual responsibility, solidarity, patriotism, innovation, and entrepreneurship.

Organizational reputation, identity, and image

Organizational reputation, identity, and image are distinct yet interrelated constructs. Organizational reputation is generally understood as the perception held by various stakeholders (e.g., customers, employees, and investors) regarding an organization's conduct, legitimacy, authority, and ability to deliver valued outcomes. This perception influences stakeholders' trust, customer loyalty, and overall organizational success (Dominic et al., 2024). It encompasses stakeholders' overall assessments of the organization's characteristics, credibility, trustworthiness, actions, achievements, and standing (Baruah & Panda, 2020; Gioia et al., 2014).

Reputation is closely related to organizational identity, both of which are considered essential for organizational success (Whetten &

DOI: 10.4324/9781003368366-3

Mackey, 2002). While organizational identity refers to the collective understanding and perception of an organization's values, beliefs, goals, and purpose by its internal stakeholders (Freeman & Koçak, 2023), focusing on the self-perceptions and narratives constructed by the organization, reputation reflects stakeholder feedback on the credibility of these claims. In this way, identity and reputation are interdependent: "corporate reputation is the evaluation and assessment of organizational identity, and organizational identity incorporates reputational feedback" (Huang-Horowitz, 2015, p. 347).

As for image, it refers to stakeholders' perceptions and feelings about the organization, shaped by their experiences and communications (Bozkurt, 2018). According to Laskin (2024),

> An image of an organization is a reflection of the organization's identity in the eyes of a particular public or stakeholder. If identity is how the organization wants to be seen, an image is how the organization is actually seen.
>
> (p. 6)

Image is also different from reputation, since reputation is a broader concept than image, reflecting the long-term esteem an organization earns through consistent performance and stakeholder interactions (Kuranovic, 2018). In other words, while organizational identity represents how an organization perceives itself, organizational image captures how external stakeholders view the organization, and reputation results from the long-term evaluations of its behavior, performance, reliability, and integrity.

Effective management of organizational reputation requires aligning these three elements and embedding reputational concerns into core business functions. It involves maintaining, enhancing, monitoring, adapting, and restoring this valuable asset, which significantly influences legitimacy, authority, and power (Bechan, 2022). This process is essential for organizations from the public, nonprofit, and private sectors, as it directly impacts organizational outputs, processes, and behavior.

Public relations and research on reputation management

Public relations research extensively examines the role of public relations in shaping and sustaining organizational reputation, highlighting its strategic significance in fostering goodwill and cultivating a positive organizational image. A strong reputation is portrayed as essential for achieving organizational objectives, including maintaining a competitive advantage, enhancing productivity, fostering customer loyalty, contributing to financial success, strengthening social standing, and attaining other critical outcomes (Heckert, Boumans & Vliegenhart, 2020; Huang-Horowitz & Freberg, 2016; Laskin, 2024; Lee, 2022; Romenti, 2013).

Research has identified several key factors that contribute to building and maintaining a positive organizational reputation, including ethical practices, corporate social responsibility (CSR), effective communication, stakeholder engagement, transparency, integrity, trust, and credibility (Dutot & Castellano, 2015; Etikan, 2024; Huang-Horowitz, 2015; Romenti, 2013; Yan et al., 2022). These factors have been examined in various contexts and reputation-related challenges, such as the rise of social media and stakeholders' engagement in impression management on digital platforms (Avidar, 2017, 2021; Dijkmans et al., 2015; Ji et al., 2017; Li, 2016; Yi-Ru et al., 2020), online activism (Ji et al., 2017; Li, 2016), stakeholder relationship management (Tiong, 2022), CSR strategies (Verčič & Ćorić, 2018; Wong & Dhanesh, 2017; Yan et al., 2022), and crisis management (Armutlu, 2024; Coombs, 2014; Nuortimo et al., 2024; Sohn & Lariscy, 2015). These studies underscore the complexity of reputation building and management and its dependence on consistent, ethical practices across diverse stakeholder interactions and contexts.

While public relations is widely acknowledged as central to building and managing organizational reputation, a review of the literature highlights a notable gap in addressing the cultural context in which reputation building takes place. Most studies are rooted in a U.S.-European perspective, offering limited consideration of the cultural factors that shape reputation building in other regions. This chapter seeks to fill this gap by integrating cultural factors from the GPRF into the process of organizational reputation building, using the Israeli context as a case study.

Cultural factors and organizational reputation

Cultural factors play a critical role in shaping organizational reputation, influencing both its construction and stakeholder perceptions. Perceptions of reputation vary across cultural contexts, underscoring the importance of accounting for cultural nuances in reputation management (Wang & Barajas, 2024). The relationship between culture and organizational reputation is deeply rooted in societal values, beliefs, norms, and practices, which significantly impact an organization's standing and its ability to manage its reputation effectively.

Cultural values shape stakeholder expectations regarding ethical, responsible, and commendable behavior. For example, in cultures that prioritize sustainability, organizations with strong environmental practices are more likely to cultivate a favorable reputation (Ichdan & Maryani, 2024). Additionally, cultural contexts influence how trust and credibility are established—some cultures emphasize personal relationships, while others value institutional certifications or transparent communication (Dhanesh & Avidar, 2023).

Cultural factors also affect communication strategies, including the choice of communication channels, tone, and narratives (Ahern et al., 2023). The use of culturally appropriate language, symbols, and alignment with local practices is essential for effective branding and reputation management (Jiménez & San-Martín, 2016; Wang & Barajas, 2024). For instance, Indian advertising often integrates cultural elements to strengthen emotional connections with consumers (Limbu & Mukherjee, 2024). Similarly, in China, government communication strategies for nuclear power projects are adapted to local cultural contexts to increase public acceptance (Guo & He, 2024). These cultural considerations are fundamental to understanding and managing organizational reputation. They shape stakeholder perceptions and require organizations to align with local values and expectations. Effective reputation management in a global context demands a keen awareness of cultural factors and the ability to navigate them successfully (Wang & Barajas, 2024).

While research on organizational reputation building in different cultural contexts exists, it can be further developed by integrating a broader range of cultural variables into the process. This chapter will examine the relationship between organizational reputation and cultural factors in the Israeli context through the GPRF framework.

The Israeli cultural context and the GPRF framework

To better understand organizational reputation in the Israeli cultural context, it is necessary to examine the various cultural factors that characterize Israel, as outlined in the GPRF framework. While

Chapter 2 examined the Israeli political system, religion, and activism, this chapter will focus on the economic system, societal and organizational culture, and the media system. It is important to note, however, that although these five cultural features are discussed individually, they are interconnected, each shaping and being shaped by the others.

Economic system: The "start-up nation"

Since its establishment, Israel's economy has undergone significant transformations, evolving from a socialist-oriented framework to a liberalized, market-driven model, particularly following the 1985 Economic Stabilization Program (Ben-Bassat, 2002; Plaut, 2016; Rivlin, 2016). Today, Israel operates as a mixed economy, combining substantial government involvement in key sectors with a high level of entrepreneurial activity (Shachmurove, 2019). Despite its economic success, a noticeable cognitive dissonance exists between this prosperity and the everyday economic mindset of most Israelis, who remain skeptical of the merits of economic liberalism (Plaut, 2016).

Globalization has played a crucial role in shaping Israel's modern economy, driving trade, foreign direct investment, and technological innovation. The expansion of the venture capital industry in the 1990s transformed the high-tech sector from a defense-oriented industry into a thriving start-up ecosystem, bolstered by the close relationship between the Israeli military and the tech industry (Plaut, 2016; Swed & Butler, 2015). Indeed, military service often equips individuals with essential skills and networks, fostering entrepreneurship. Additionally, the arrival of highly skilled immigrants, particularly after the collapse of the Soviet Union, significantly enhanced productivity and innovation (Razin, 2018).

Israel's economic dynamism is reflected in its reputation as the "start-up nation," driven by innovation and resilience despite challenges such as limited natural resources, geopolitical tensions, and regional disparities. Notably, the country avoided economic contraction during the 2007 global financial crisis, maintaining inflation and unemployment rates more favorable than those in the United States and Western Europe (Plaut, 2016). Its unique culture, characterized by flat hierarchies and informality, has further contributed to this entrepreneurial spirit (Senor & Singer, 2011).

Nevertheless, significant challenges persist. Internal regional disparities and a digital divide highlight the uneven distribution of economic prosperity. Urban centers like Tel Aviv and Jerusalem enjoy superior infrastructure and economic opportunities, while peripheral regions such as the Negev and Galilee—home to many Israeli Arab citizens—struggle with lower income levels, inadequate infrastructure, and reduced access to resources, exacerbating societal tensions (Haddad et al., 2022). The digital divide in the Israeli economy is characterized by significant disparities in access to and utilization of digital technologies, which are influenced by socioeconomic, regional, and ethnic factors. In Israel, ethnic disparities are particularly pronounced in the utilization of digital healthcare services, with the Jewish majority exhibiting higher usage rates and more positive attitudes toward these services compared to the Arab minority. This disparity is partly attributed to differences in digital health literacy and attitudes, which are stronger predictors of digital service utilization among the Jewish population (Obeid et al., 2023).

In summary, Israel's transformation into a global leader in high-tech industries underscores the impact of globalization, innovation, and entrepreneurship. However, addressing persistent disparities and fostering inclusive growth will require a nuanced understanding of the interplay between Israel's cultural context and its economic development.

Societal and organizational culture: Foundational cultural principles

Israeli society is a multifaceted blend of religions, ethnicities, cultures, and political ideologies. This diversity, while enriching the nation's collective identity, has also given rise to significant social divides. These rifts are particularly evident in the realms of religion, politics, and socio-economic status, rooted in historical developments, entrenched narratives, and ongoing conflicts (Akerman & Garma, 2023). Israel's population encompasses a wide range of cultural and ethnic communities, including Jewish, Arab, Druze, and Christian groups. The Jewish community itself reflects substantial ethnic and religious heterogeneity, with pronounced distinctions among Orthodox, traditional, and secular segments. Over the past few decades, the growing polarization between ultra-Orthodox and secular Jews, coupled with the shrinking traditional middle ground, has led to notable changes in patterns of religious identification (Rebhun, 2023).

Ethnicity and religious practices deeply influence individual and collective identities, shaping attitudes and behaviors across Israeli society. This interplay of factors creates a vibrant yet occasionally contentious social dynamic (Lewin-Epstein & Cohen, 2019; Rebhun, 2023). In such a culturally diverse environment, public communications—whether corporate or political—must carefully navigate a web of expectations and sensitivities. Organizations operating in this context must integrate cultural norms and values into their strategies to effectively build their identity, enhance their reputation, and sustain a favorable public image.

One of the foundational principles of Israeli culture is *mutual responsibility* (*Arvut Hadadit*) and *solidarity*, deeply embedded in Jewish philosophy and the societal ethos (Rosenthal, 2014; Sassoni-Bar-Lev & Avidar, 2023a; 2023b). These values, rooted in the historical and cultural experiences of the Jewish people, emphasize mutual aid, communal welfare, and shared responsibility. Beyond their religious and philosophical origins, they serve as practical foundations for community life and civil society. This ethos is reflected in various aspects of Israeli society, from the kibbutzim communal settlements to widespread practices of volunteering and philanthropy. Israeli culture reinforces these ideals through shared goals, loyalty, collective action, and personal sacrifice, as well as a strong commitment to helping those in need (Rosenthal, 2014; Tikochinsky, 2014).

In recent years, *mutual responsibility* and *solidarity* in Israel have faced growing challenges due to increasing divisions along religious, financial, political, ethnic, and national lines (Sassoni-Bar-Lev & Avidar, 2023a; 2023b). While the COVID-19 pandemic further highlighted these fractures (Gilbar & Karako-Eyal, 2023), the controversial "judicial reform" initiative introduced in 2023 by Prime Minister Benjamin Netanyahu's right-wing government had a far greater impact. Aimed at weakening the Supreme Court and altering the balance of power among Israel's executive, legislative, and judicial branches, the reform intensified societal tensions and sparked mass protests across the country. This political turmoil, marked by the largest demonstrations in Israel's history, exposed deep societal divides and fears for the nation's democratic principles (Gidron & Katz, 2024). However, the Hamas attack on Israel on October 7, 2023, and the subsequent war demonstrated the enduring strength of solidarity within Israeli society. Civil society organizations, including those previously focused on protests and others not, quickly mobilized to provide essential services to populations in need across various regions. These efforts included collecting personal equipment for reserve soldiers, providing clothing for evacuees from towns and kibbutzim near the Gaza Strip and the North, organizing transportation for those requiring evacuation, and more—all stepping in voluntarily where the public sector proved slow and ineffective (Gidron & Katz, 2024). This "liberal serving elite" (Gidron & Katz, 2024) highlights both the ideological and political divides within Israeli society and the resilience of solidarity as a core cultural value, particularly during times of national crisis. Despite these divisions, solidarity remains a key part of Israeli identity.

In the business sector, solidarity extends beyond profit-making, encompassing shared ideas about collective values and interests. This approach can enhance the reputation of businesses by portraying them as collegial and community-oriented rather than solely profit-driven (Spillman, 2012). Moreover, when strategically employed, solidarity can play a significant role in reputation building by fostering trust, cooperation, and a commitment to equity and community well-being (Moore et al., 2023).

Patriotism is another central cultural value in Israel, encompassing emotional, cognitive, and social dimensions that reflect an individual's deep love and loyalty to their homeland. This relationship often involves a strong commitment to the country's values, traditions, and well-being (Johnston, 2014). Research indicates that corporations cultivating a patriotic brand image can boost local consumers' purchase intentions by emphasizing perceived quality, corporate ability, integrity, and social responsibility (Li et al., 2021). Corporate patriotism plays a pivotal role in shaping corporate reputation, particularly by enhancing perceptions of the company as a responsible local citizen in employer and community relationships (Puncheva-Michelotti et al., 2014). In the Israeli context, both domestic and international corporations that align with patriotic values—such as supporting the Israeli military or promoting Israeli innovation—can significantly enhance their reputations and strengthen relationships with strategic publics. The Israeli defense industry, a cornerstone of the nation's innovation success, positively influences the reputation of associated organizations (Yeshua-Katz & Efrat-Treister, 2021). As a result, brands that support the military or engage in causes aligned with national interests tend to resonate deeply with the public.

Conversely, actions perceived as conflicting with patriotism and national values—such as affiliations with movements viewed as anti-Israel—can damage an organization's reputation. For example, nongovernmental organizations (NGOs) involved in human rights issues related to the Arab-Israeli conflict, particularly those perceived as promoting anti-Israel agendas, often face skepticism and criticism from the Israeli public. Such organizations are frequently viewed as biased, focusing disproportionately on Israel while downplaying security threats and terrorism (Steinberg, 2009). Media coverage of these activities can further influence stakeholder perceptions, potentially amplifying reputational harm if an organization is seen as opposing national interests (Reuber & Fischer, 2010). As a result, Israeli organizations must carefully navigate their actions and affiliations to protect their reputations amid both national and international scrutiny.

Finally, *innovation and entrepreneurship* are highly valued in Israeli culture, which proudly identifies with its reputation as the "start-up nation" (Schäfer & Henn, 2023). Israeli organizations that foster a culture of innovation and deliver cutting-edge solutions can enhance their reputation by positioning themselves as leaders in progress. This start-up mindset strengthens the perception of Israeli companies as flexible, forward-thinking, and highly adaptable. Even organizations outside the high-tech sector often adopt "high-tech marketing" strategies to project a more innovative and glamorous image, thereby attracting investors, clients, and employees (Mashiah, 2022). According to Mashiah (2022), the Israeli high-tech industry enjoys extensive, positive, and consistent media coverage, bolstering its reputation as the "start-up nation." This reputation is fueled by the public's enthusiasm for innovation, proactive public relations efforts, and journalists' favorable treatment of the industry, which collectively contribute to its societal glorification and admiration.

In summary, the cultural values of Israeli society—such as mutual responsibility, solidarity, patriotism, innovation, and entrepreneurship—play a crucial role in shaping how organizations build and manage their reputations. The country's complex and diverse social landscape, marked by significant divisions along religious, ethnic, and political lines, requires organizations to carefully navigate these cultural dynamics. To succeed in this multifaceted environment, both Israeli and international organizations must align with the country's core cultural values—whether by fostering innovation, supporting national interests, or demonstrating solidarity and mutual responsibility. By doing so, organizations can not only enhance their reputations but also forge stronger connections with Israeli stakeholders in this unique and dynamic societal context.

The media system: A changing media landscape

The Israeli media system is a complex structure shaped by history, politics, and technology. It has evolved through distinct phases, from early British colonial influence to the modern digital age, characterized by rapid technological advancements and a decline in print media (Neiger, 2023). This evolution reflects a mix of European and British influences, blending authoritarian elements like military censorship with democratic principles such as freedom of the press, even though this freedom is not constitutionally guaranteed (Nossek, 2007).

A defining feature of Israel's media landscape is its combination of diversity and centralization. A small number of dominant media outlets, including public broadcasters like the Israel Broadcasting Corporation (Kan), commercial TV channels such as Channels 12 and 13, and leading newspapers like *Haaretz*, *Yedioth Ahronoth*, *Ma'ariv*, and *Israel Hayom*, hold significant sway over news dissemination and public discourse (Ha'ayin Hashvi'it, 2021). Despite concerns about media bias and the influence of political and business interests, the Israeli media remains vibrant, with a strong tradition of investigative journalism and a wide range of viewpoints. Competition among outlets, as Gentzkow and Shapiro (2008) note, helps mitigate bias by ensuring that multiple perspectives are represented, fostering a more independent media environment.

Since the early 2000s, the Israeli media environment has transitioned into a multichannel, digital era driven by broadband internet (Neiger, 2023). Traditional media outlets, such as print, radio, and television, have adapted by developing robust online presences through websites and mobile apps, reaching broader audiences. Meanwhile, online-only publications and alternative news platforms have emerged, providing diverse perspectives and catering to niche audiences during both routine periods and national crises (Malka et al., 2015).

Digital platforms and social media have further reshaped Israel's media landscape, offering new ways to share news and organizational messages. Platforms like Facebook, X (formerly Twitter), and Instagram facilitate direct interaction between journalists, media organizations, and the public (Neiger, 2023). Social media is particularly popular in Israel, with YouTube and WhatsApp each boasting a 98% usage rate, followed by Facebook at 87% (Israel Internet Association, 2024). This hyper-connected environment enables the rapid dissemination of messages and fosters public mobilization and engagement around various issues. Israeli public discourse, known for its directness and openness (Katriel, 1986), often escalates on social media, amplifying controversies, particularly when cultural, religious, or political sensitivities arise (Katriel, 2018; Sassoni-Bar Lev & Avidar, 2023b).

The media system in Israel reflects a blend of public, private, and limited international ownership. Most major outlets, including newspapers and television channels, are privately owned and commercially funded, relying heavily on advertising revenue (Ha'ayin Hashvi'it, 2021). Public broadcasting, represented by Kan and Galei Tzahal (Israel Defense Forces Radio), remains influential, especially in national news coverage. Although freedom of the press is legally protected, debates occasionally arise about media ownership concentration and its potential to suppress diverse voices. Critics argue that political and business interests may affect news coverage, yet Israel's media environment remains robust, with journalists frequently exposing corruption and holding power to account (Freedom House, 2024).

The Israeli media also plays a critical role in shaping organizational image and reputation, particularly through its handling of cultural sensitivities. In a society marked by diverse religious, ethnic, and political groups, media representations can significantly influence public perceptions of organizations. Organizational communications that disregard cultural nuances or violate societal norms risk provoking backlash, especially on social media, where public reactions are swift and widespread (Han, 2024). In conclusion, the Israeli media system plays a crucial role in shaping organizational reputation. Its dynamic mix of public, private, and digital platforms offers opportunities for engagement and message amplification but also increases scrutiny. To maintain a favorable reputation, organizations must strategically engage with the media while navigating cultural sensitivities in Israel's diverse society.

A culturally embedded organizational reputation model

Organizational reputation is a valuable asset shaped by the collective perceptions and judgments of both external and internal stakeholders.

It emerges from the interaction between organizational characteristics and the surrounding cultural context, as outlined in the GPRF framework. This chapter introduces a *culturally embedded organizational reputation model* (CEORM) that integrates "culture" into the process of reputation building to provide a more comprehensive and culturally relevant framework. A case study is also presented to demonstrate the application of this approach.

The CEORM includes the following constructs:

1. *Cultural Integration and Responsiveness*
   Cultural integration and responsiveness refer to the sensitivity with which organizations incorporate cultural awareness into their reputation-building practices. This requires understanding, respecting, and responding to the cultural context in which they operate while acknowledging public sentiment and aligning organizational behavior with societal expectations. It also involves value-driven communication, ensuring that organizational messages reflect core cultural values that resonate with both internal and external stakeholders. In the Israeli context, such values include mutual responsibility, solidarity, patriotism, innovation, and entrepreneurship. For instance, many Israeli companies strive to cultivate a "high-tech," innovative reputation, knowing that Israelis admire the glamorous image of the high-tech industry (Mashiah, 2022).
2. *Political and Economic Adaptability*
   Political and economic adaptability requires organizations to strategically navigate local political and economic constraints to avoid reputational risks. In the Israeli context, this involves aligning with the country's fragmented political landscape and economic disparities while maintaining a balance between neutrality and sensitivity to political and societal issues. Successful organizations either actively support national causes or skillfully steer clear of controversies. For example, organizations that align with national causes—such as supporting the Israel Defense Forces (IDF), especially during times of war and national crises, or contributing to the nation's innovation ecosystem—can gain public trust and loyalty and enhance their reputation (Yeshua-Katz & Efrat-Treister, 2021).
3. *Media Savviness*
   Media savviness reflects an organization's ability to strategically navigate media platforms by understanding their cultural dynamics, such as openness, political orientation, target audiences,

and preferred content types. This involves tailoring messages to specific publics (e.g., religious, secular, Jewish, Arab) to maximize relevance and impact. It also includes responding effectively to negative coverage or crises at both organizational and national levels, as exemplified by targeted financial advertising during the "Swords of Iron" war (Blitz, Roth-Cohen, & Avraham, 2024). Additionally, media savviness requires staying current by adapting to emerging trends, influencers, audience preferences, digitalization, and new technologies to ensure communication strategies remain effective and relevant. By aligning communication efforts with the cultural and societal context, media savviness directly influences the way an organization builds its image and reputation. In order to do so, organizations need to remain flexible and adjust their communication strategies to reflect changes in the socio-political and cultural landscape. They also have to regularly monitor social sentiment through digital platforms and media coverage to anticipate potential reputational risks and respond proactively. Since the Israeli public is highly engaged in social media, where reputational crises can escalate rapidly, organizations need a proactive strategy for digital engagement, using social media to build and sustain their reputations.

4 *Co-Creation and Meaningful Engagement with stakeholders*
Co-creation and meaningful engagement with stakeholders mean that organizations co-create their reputation by engaging with internal and external stakeholders, such as customers, employees, community leaders, and media professionals. Co-creation helps organizations maintain their reputation as relevant in a rapidly shifting cultural and political landscape. For example, a recent campaign launched in 2024 by leaders of Israeli industry and major companies, titled "Continuing to Live Together," aimed to engage the Israeli public to prevent societal escalation and create a shared foundation for economic and social prosperity in the aftermath of the Swords of Iron War. The campaign brought together Jewish and Arab entrepreneurs, industrialists, researchers, teachers, doctors, and actors to discuss the challenges and complexities of the current situation and to share their feelings and experiences of living together (Calcalist, 2024). This effort to engage the Israeli public in a discourse of tolerance and unity also enabled the participating organizations to project a positive image and build a favorable reputation as promoters of inclusiveness and unity.

To summarize, the CEORM framework offers a comprehensive approach to understanding how organizations can build and manage their reputations by integrating cultural, political, economic, activist, and media-related factors. This model underscores the importance of cultural sensitivity, national alignment, and stakeholder engagement in creating reputations that are resilient and adaptive to unique social dynamics. By applying the CEORM, organizations can effectively navigate Israel's complex and multifaceted cultural landscape to build a positive reputation. Moreover, this approach provides a model for organizations globally to engage more meaningfully with the communities they serve, potentially prompting a broader rethinking of what defines a successful and positive organizational reputation.

Case study: Reputation building by Israeli banks during the Swords of Iron War

Advertising campaigns for Israeli banks illustrate the connection between organizational reputation and the GPRF and CEORM frameworks. Historically, the Israeli banking sector has struggled to maintain a positive reputation, particularly after the 1983 banking crisis, which eroded perceptions of fairness, service quality, and trust (Kidron & Kreis, 2022; Shenkar & Yuchtman-Yaar, 1986). This crisis created an urgent need for trust and reputation repair, prompting banks to focus on transparency and consistency to rebuild consumer confidence (Kidron & Kreis, 2022). Recent data from a household survey showed that only 54% of Israeli bank customers feel their bank treats them fairly, a slight drop from 55% in 2022 (Bank of Israel, 2024). These numbers indicate persistent dissatisfaction and negative sentiment among customers regarding banks' fairness and service quality, which intensifies when annual reports of high bank profits are published (e.g., Green, 2024). To address these challenges, Israeli banks, like other corporations, utilize advertising campaigns—particularly on TV and social media—to strengthen their public image and build a more positive reputation. These campaigns often incorporate Israeli cultural and societal values, aiming to evoke feelings of home, familiarity, and belonging, while also addressing financial concerns and societal divides (Lavie-Dinur & Karniel, 2019).

The Swords of Iron War between Israel and Hamas, which began on October 7, 2023, presented a tragic yet significant opportunity for Israeli banks to demonstrate *political and economic adaptability*, align with the severe security situation, and build a more positive reputation by actively supporting national and social causes. A recent study (Blitz, Roth-Cohen & Avraham, 2024) found that during the first 100 days of the war, Israeli financial institutions focused their advertising campaigns on Israeli cultural values, such as collectivism, solidarity, generosity, patriotism, and tradition. These campaigns featured symbols of national pride—flags, landscapes, familiar icons, and well-known songs—that appealed to emotions and evoked nostalgia, fostering trust and loyalty. One notable example is a commercial by The Israel International Bank, which used the iconic Israeli song "*Lo tenatzu oti*" ("*You will not defeat me*") while the presenter spoke directly to the camera about the bank's financial assistance to soldiers and their families. The scenes depicted families concerned for their loved ones serving in the army, creating an emotional, engaging, and easily understood narrative (The Israel International Bank, 2023).

In line with the CEORM framework, Israeli banks leveraged *media savviness, co-creation, and meaningful stakeholder engagement* through traditional and social media platforms to address issues such as regulatory information, assistance for soldiers on reserve and their families, community involvement, and other critical concerns. These efforts aimed to build a responsible and patriotic reputation (Blitz, Roth-Cohen & Avraham, 2024). The banks also demonstrated *cultural integration and responsiveness* by aligning organizational behavior with societal expectations and acknowledging public sentiment. Campaigns emphasized patriotism, national unity, pride, and public trust, with messaging focused on supporting the IDF and engaging in CSR initiatives. These initiatives included aiding vulnerable populations affected by the war, such as families of Israeli hostages and residents evacuated from southern and northern borders. For instance, Mizrahi-Tefahot Bank contributed millions of shekels for equipment for Gaza border residents, soldiers, and volunteers, including food, clothing, emergency kits, and defense equipment. Bank employees also volunteered to pack meals for soldiers and civilians in the south (Kikar Hashabat & Mizrahi-Tefahot, 2023). Promoted via television and social media platforms, these efforts sought to foster public engagement and enhance the socially-aware reputation of Israeli banks. Overall, this case study demonstrates that organizational reputation building is a co-creational process that integrates culture and cultural elements to enhance and promote a positive reputation.

Questions for further discussion

1 How do cultural values and societal expectations influence organizational reputation building, and what role do these factors play in various cultural contexts?
2 How can organizations incorporate national identity and cultural norms into their communication strategies to enhance their reputation? How might these approaches differ across cultures?
3 What are the key challenges organizations face in balancing local cultural sensitivity with global reputation management? How can they address these complexities effectively?
4 How do culturally diverse environments shape the way organizations build and maintain their reputation through traditional and social media?

References

Ahern, S., Marshall, S., Wallbank, G., Jawad, D., Taki, S., Baur, L.A., & Wen, L.M. (2023). Communication strategies and effectiveness of early childhood obesity-related prevention programs for linguistically diverse communities: A rapid review. *Obesity Reviews, 24*(12), e13634. https://doi.org/10.1111/obr.13634

Akerman, L., & Garma, H. (2023). *Position paper: Polarization and divisions in Israeli society*. Reichman University, The Institute for Policy and Strategy (IPS). [Hebrew]. www.runi.ac.il/media/3pzlljwb/lior27-3-24.pdf.

Armutlu, I.I. (2024). Corporate reputation and crisis management in social media: The Patiswiss case study, *International Journal of Research and Innovation in Social Science, 8*(9), 682–692 https://doi.org/10.47772/IJRISS.2024.809061

Avidar, R. (2017). Public relations and social businesses: The importance of enhancing engagement. *Public Relations Review, 43*(5), 955–962. https://doi.org/10.1016/j.pubrev.2017.03.015

Avidar, R. (2021). The challenge of building a favorable reputation for social businesses. *Social Business, 11*(1–2), 80–99(20). https://doi.org/10.1362/204440821X16206324311178

Bank of Israel (2024, March 19). The Banking Supervision Department publishes the findings of the annual survey on the satisfaction of household customers and business owners with the service provided to them by the banks. *Press Releases*. [Hebrew]. www.boi.org.il/publications/pressreleases/19-03-24/

Baruah, L., & Panda, N.M. (2020). Measuring corporate reputation: A comprehensive model with enhanced objectivity. *Asia-Pacific Journal of Business Administration, 12*(2), 139–161. https://doi.org/10.1108/APJBA-10-2019-0215

Bechan, N. (2022). Top determinants of corporate reputation management. *Communicare: Journal for Communication Studies in Africa, 27*(1–2), 1–18. https://doi.org/10.36615/jcsa.v27i1-2.1738

Ben-Bassat, A. (2002). *The Israeli economy, 1985–1998: From government intervention to market economics*. MIT Press.

Blitz, E., Roth-Cohen, O., & Avraham, E. (2024). "Stronger together": Financial advertising during Swords if Iron War. *Misgarot Media*. Online First [Hebrew]. https://mediaframes.sapir.ac.il/financial-advertising/

Bozkurt, M. (2018). Corporate image, brand and reputation concepts and their importance for tourism establishments. *International Journal of Contemporary Tourism, 2*(2), 60–66. https://doi.org/10.30625/ijctr.461064

Calcalist (2024, January 8). "Continuing to live together": A new campaign featuring Jews and Arabs goes live. www.calcalist.co.il/shopping/article/s18gp6tut

Coombs, W.T. (2014). *Ongoing crisis communication: Planning, managing and responding*. Sage. ISBN: 9781071816646.

Dhanesh, G.S., & Avidar, R. (2023). Culture and dialog theory in public relations: The Middle Eastern context. In E. Sommerfeldt and C. Botan (Eds.). *Public Relations Theory III*, pp. 321–337. Routledge. ISBN: 9780367683313.

Dijkmans, O., Kerkhof, P., & Beukeboom, C.G. (2015). A stage to engage: Social media use and corporate reputation. *Tourism Management, 47*, 58–67. https://doi.org/10.1016/j.tourman.2014.09.005

Dominic, E.D., Mahamed, M., Maledo, R.O., Erica, O.A., & Obaro, J.E. (2024). Expounding organizational reputation/crisis: Exploring its definitional landscape. *International Journal of Academic Research in Business & Social Sciences, 14*(8), 937–952. http://doi.org/10.6007/IJARBSS/v14-i8/21880

Dutot, V., & Castellano, S. (2015). Designing a measurement scale for e-reputation. *Corporate Reputation Review, 18*(4), 294–313. https://doi.org/10.1057/crr.2015.15

Etikan, J. (2024). Corporate social responsibility (CSR) and its influence on organizational reputation. *Journal of Public Relations, 2*(1), 1–12. https://doi.org/10.47941/jpr.1694

Freedom House. (2024). *Expanding freedom and democracy*. https://freedomhouse.org/countries/freedom-world/scores

Freeman, A., & Koçak, Ö. (2023). Designing inclusive organizational identities. *Journal of Organization Design, 12*, 177–193. https://doi.org/10.1007/s41469-023-00150-0

Gentzkow, M., & Shapiro, J.M. (2008). Competition and truth in the market for news. *Journal of Economic Perspectives, 22*(2), 133–154. doi: 10.1257/JEP.22.2.133

Gidron, B., & Katz, H. (2024). Israel's civil society 2023 from protest to aid provision – a serving elite perspective. *Frontiers in Sociology*, *9*. https://doi.org/10.3389/fsoc.2024.1417687

Gilbar, R., & Karako-Eyal, N. (2023). Beyond authority and governance in Israel during the COVID-19 pandemic: A crumbling of solidarity and the rise of social inequalities. In S. Germain and A. Yong (Eds.). *Beyond the Virus: Multidisciplinary and International Perspectives on Inequalities Raised by COVID-19*, pp. 34–55. Bristol University Press. https://doi.org/10.46692/9781529221268.005

Gioia, D.A., Hamilton, A.L., & Patvardhan, S.D. (2014). Image is everything: Reflections on the dominance of image in modern organizational life. *Research in Organizational Behavior*, *34*, 129–154. https://doi.org/10.1016/j.riob.2014.01.001

Green, S. (2024, August 17). This is how the banks managed to maintain huge profits despite the war. *Calcalist*. [Hebrew]. www.calcalist.co.il/market/article/bkhyhq09r

Guo, Y., & He, L. (2024). Communicating in diverse local cultures: Analyzing Chinese government communication programs around nuclear power projects. *Review of Policy Research, 41*(4), 654–658. https://doi.org/10.1111/ropr.12576

Ha'ayin Hashvi'it (The Seventh Eye) (2021). *Ownership map of the Israeli media*. [Hebrew]. www.the7eye.org.il/50534

Haddad, H.Y.N., Khalaila, M., Rudnitzky, A., & Farjun, B. (2022). *The yearbook of Arab society in Israel.* The Israel Democracy Institute. [Hebrew].

Han, Z. (2024). The role and influence of social media in crisis communication: An analysis with Twitter as an example. *Lecture Notes in Education Psychology and Public Media, 54*(1), 87–95. https://doi.org/10.54254/2753-7048/54/20241609

Heckert, R., Boumans, J., & Vliegenthart, R. (2020). How to nail the multiple identities of an organization? A content analysis of projected identity. *Voluntas*, *31*, 129–141. https://doi.org/10.1007/s11266-019-00157-w

Huang-Horowitz, N.C. (2015). Public relations in the small business environment: Creating identity and building reputation. *Public Relations Review*, *41*, 345–353. https://doi.org/10.1016/j.pubrev.2014.10.018

Huang-Horowitz, N.C., & Freberg, K. (2016). Bridging organizational identity and reputation messages online: A conceptual model. *Corporate Communications: An International Journal, 21*(2), 195–212. https://doi.org/10.1108/CCIJ-06-2014-0034

Ichdan, D.A., & Maryani, M. (2024). The impact of innovation, corporate social responsibility, environmental practices, and organizational culture on organizational sustainability. *Annals of Management and Organization Research, 5*(4), 297–310. https://doi.org/10.35912/amor.v5i4.2236

Israel Internet Association (2024). *Social media and online services usage in Israel: 2024 data with demographic breakdowns*. [Hebrew]. www.isoc.org.il/sts-data/online_services_index

Ji, W.J., Li, C., North, M., & Liu, J. (2017). Staking reputation on stakeholders: How does stakeholders Facebook engagement help or ruin a company's reputation? *Public Relations Review, 43*(1), 201–210. https://doi.org/10.1016/j.pubrev.2016.12.004

Jiménez, N., & San-Martín, S. (2016). The central role of the reputation of country-of-origin firms in developing markets. *Journal of Business & Industrial Marketing, 31*(3), 349–364. https://doi.org/10.1108/JBIM-02-2013-0045

Johnston, S. (2014). Patriotism. *The Encyclopedia of Political Thought*, 2673–2682. https://doi.org/10.1002/9781118474396.wbept0758

Katriel, T. (1986). *Talking straight: Dugri speech in Israeli sabra culture*. Cambridge University Press. ISBN-13: 978-0-52132-630-8

Katriel, T. (2018). Accounts and rebuttals in an Israeli discourse of dissent. *Journal of Multicultural Discourses, 13*(1), 1–16. https://doi.org/10.1080/17447143.2017.1405963

Kidron, A., & Kreis, Y. (2022). Restoring trust after banks crisis: the Israeli case study. *Israel Affairs*, *28*(3), 484–500. https://doi.org/10.1080/13537121.2022.2066865

Kikar Hashabat & Mizrahi-Tefahot (October 12, 2023). Mizrahi-Tefahot offers a package of benefits and relief measures in light of the war. *Kikar-Hashabat*. [Hebrew]. www.kikar.co.il/%D7%AA%D7%9B% D7%A0%D7%95%D7%9F-%D7%9E%D7%A9%D7%9B%D7%A0%D7%AA%D7%90%D7%95%D7%AA/442229

Kuranovic, V. (2018). Research analysis of Chinas corporate identity image and reputation. *Business Studies Journal, 9*(1), 2018.

Laskin, A.V. (2024). *Organizational reputation management: A strategic public relations perspective*. Wiley-Blackwell. ISBN: 978-1-394-18033-2.

Lavie-Dinur, A., & Karniel, Y. (2019). An examination of changing values in Israeli television commercials between 2012 and 2016. *Advertising & Society Quarterly, 20*(1). https://doi.org/10.1353/asr.2019.0002.

Lee, J.W. (2022). Impacts of public relations on corporate reputation. *Journal of Digital Marketing and Communication, 2*(1), 30–36. https://doi.org/10.53623/jdmc.v2i1.82

Lewin-Epstein, N., & Cohen, Y. (2019). Ethnic origin and identity in the Jewish population of Israel. *Journal of Ethnic and Migration Studies, 45*(11), 2118–2137. https://doi.org/10.1080/1369183X.2018.1492370

Li, Y., Teng, W., Liao, T.-T., & Lin, T.M.Y. (2021). Exploration of patriotic brand image: Its antecedents and impacts on purchase intentions. *Asia Pacific Journal of Marketing and Logistics, 33*(6), 1455–1481. https://doi.org/10.1108/APJML-11-2019-0660

Li, Z. (2016). Psychological empowerment on social media: Who are the empowered users? *Public Relations Review, 42*(1), 49–59. https://doi.org/10.1016/j.pubrev.2015.09.001

Limbu, S., & Mukherjee, D.K. (2024). Cultural attributes in advertising: An Indian perspective. *Educational Administration: Theory and Practice, 30*(1), 1128–1136. https://doi.org/10.53555/kuey.v30i1.5988

Malka, V., Ariel, Y., & Avidar, R. (2015). Fighting, worrying and sharing: Operation 'Protective Edge' as the first WhatsApp war. *Media, War, and Conflict,* 8(3), 329–344. https://doi.org/10.1177/1750635215611610

Mashiah, I. (2022). *Communication and high-tech*. Orion. [Hebrew].

Moore, C., Nichol, A., & Taylor, H. (2023). Supporting solidarity: Public health's role in achieving social justice. *Voices in Bioethics,* 9. https://doi.org/10.52214/vib.v9i.11758

Neiger, M. (2023). Israel's media landscape: Democratic practice, constrained environment. In P.R. Kumaraswamy (Eds.). *The Palgrave International Handbook of Israel*, pp. 1–19. Palgrave Macmillan. https://doi.org/10.1007/978-981-16-2717-0

Nossek, H. (2007). Vox populi or lonely voices in the wasteland of the ionosphere: The case of Israeli community television. In L.K. Fuller (Eds.). *Community Media*, pp. 111–122. Palgrave Macmillan. https://doi.org/10.1057/9780230604872_10

Nuortimo, K., Harkonen, J., & Breznik, K. (2024). Exploring corporate reputation and crisis communication. *Journal of Marketing Analy*tics. https://doi.org/10.1057/s41270-024-00353-8

Obeid, S., Mashiach-Eizenberg, M., Gur, A., & Lavy, I. (2023). Examining ethnic disparities in digital healthcare services utilization: Insights from Israel. *Journal of Multidisciplinary Healthcare, 16*, 3533–3544. https://doi.org/10.2147/JMDH.S429121

Plaut, S. (2016). Israel's socialist dreams vs. capitalist realities. *Middle East Quarterly, 23*(3), 1–12.

Puncheva-Michelotti, P., McColl, R., Vocino, A., & Michelotti, M. (2014). Corporate patriotism as a source of corporate reputation: A comparative multi-stakeholder approach. *Journal of Strategic Marketing, 22*(6), 471–493. https://doi.org/10.1080/0965254X.2014.885989

Razin, A. (2018). *Israel and the world economy: The power of globalization*. MIT Press. ISBN: 9780262037341.

Rebhun, U. (2023). Jewish diversity in Israel. *European Judaism, 56*(2), 88–111. https://doi.org/10.3167/ej.2023.560209

Reuber, A.R., & Fischer, E. (2010). Organizations behaving badly: When are discreditable actions likely to damage organizational reputation? *Journal of Business Ethics, 93*, 39–50. https://doi.org/10.1007/s10551-009-0180-3

Rivlin, P. (2016). Stabilization and liberalization in the Israeli economy. In M. Erdoğdu and B. Christiansen (Eds.). *Handbook of Research on Comparative Economic Development Perspectives on Europe and the MENA Region*, pp. 524–540. IGI Global Scientific Publishing. https://doi.org/10.4018/978-1-4666-9548-1.ch022

Romenti, S. (2013). Reputation management: The key to successful public relations and corporate communication. *Corporate Communications, 18*(1), 161–164. https://doi.org/10.1108/13563281311294182

Rosenthal, R. (2014). Solidarity: The Hebrew version. In Y.Z. Stern and B. Porat (Eds.). *In Search of Solidarity: An Israeli Journey*, pp. 72–93. The Israel Democracy Institute. [Hebrew]. ISBN: 978-965-519-136-3

Sassoni-Bar Lev, O., & Avidar, R. (2023a). 'God forbid we'd be infected': framing and counter-framing of the 'Corona Cruise Ship' in Israeli media. *The Journal of International Communication, 29*(2), 213–233. https://doi.org/10.1080/13216597.2023.2203687

Sassoni-Bar Lev, O., & Avidar, R. (2023b). 'And parents shall come again to their own border': Belonging and solidarity in the face of exclusion and anxiety in the media coverage of the Corona Ship. In H. Hazaz-Berger, G. Yair, and T. Gamliel (Eds.). *Urgent Ethnography: Aspects and Challenges in the Corona Plague.* University of Bar-Ilan. [Hebrew]. ISBN: 978-965-226-650-7.

Schäfer, S., & Henn, S. (2023). Chapter 7: Start-up nation Israel: Transnational entrepreneurs, born globals and cross-border connections of the Israeli high-tech industry. In *Research Handbook on Transnational Diaspora Entrepreneurship.* Edward Elgar Publishing. https://doi.org/10.4337/9781788118699.00016

Senor, D., & Singer, S. (2011). *Start-up nation: The story of Israel's economic miracle.* Grand-Central Publishing.

Shachmurove, Y. (2019). Determinants of economic growth in Israel. In M. Osińska (Eds.). *Economic Miracles in the European Economies.* Springer. https://doi.org/10.1007/978-3-030-05606-3_6

Shenkar, O., & Yuchtman-Yaar, E. (1986). The image of Israeli banking. *International Journal of Bank Marketing, 4*(3), 69–80. https://doi.org/10.1108/eb010785

Sohn, Y.J., & Lariscy, R.W. (2015). A buffer or boomerang—The role of corporate reputation in bad times. *Communication Research, 42*(2), 237–259. https://doi.org/10.1177/0093650212466891

Spillman, L. (2012). *Solidarity in strategy.* University of Chicago Press Economics Books. University of Chicago Press.

Steinberg, G.M. (2009). The centrality of Ngos in promoting anti-Israel boycotts and sanctions. *Jewish Political Studies Review, 21*(1/2), 7–31.

Swed, O., & Butler, J.S. (2015). Military capital in the Israeli hi-tech industry. *Armed Forces & Society, 41(1),* 123–141. https://doi.org/10.1177/0095327X13499562

The Israel International Bank [FIBI Bank] (2023, December 10). A fund of 100 million NIS for interest-free loans and mortgage benefits for career soldiers [Video]. *YouTube.* [Hebrew]. www.youtube.com/watch?v=MIy9WBivYMg.

Tikochinsky, M. (2014). And the redemptive came from near: On fraternity and redemption." In Y.Z. Stern and B. Porat (Eds.). *In search of Solidarity: An Israeli Journey*, pp. 217–242. The Israel Democracy Institute. [Hebrew]. ISBN: 978-965-519-136-3.

Tiong, A.C-.C. (2022). Corporate reputation: Building and maintaining. *Journal of Digital Marketing and Communication, 2*(1), 25–29. https://doi.org/10.53623/jdmc.v2i1.96

Verčič, A.T., & Ćorić, D.S. (2018). The relationship between reputation, employer branding and corporate social responsibility. *Public Relations Review*, *44*, 444–452. https://doi.org/10.1016/j.pubrev.2018.06.005

Wang, F., & Barajas, Á. (2024). Influence of cultural factors on organizational performance of multinational corporations: A bibliometric review from 1983 to 2020. *Qeios, 6*(8). https://doi.org/10.32388/C37MQ5.3

Whetten, D.A., & Mackey, A. (2002). A social actor conception of organizational identity and its implications for the study of organizational reputation. *Business & Society*, *41*, 393–414. https://doi.org/10.1177/0007650302238775

Wong, J.Y., & Dhanesh, G.S. (2017). Communicating corporate social responsibility (CSR) in the luxury industry: Managing CSR–luxury paradox online through acceptance strategies of coexistence and convergence. *Management Communication Quarterly, 31*(1), 88–112. https://doi.org/10.1177/0893318916669602

Yan, X., Espinosa-Cristia, J.F., Kumari, K., & Cioca, L.I. (2022). Relationship between corporate social responsibility, organizational trust, and corporate reputation for sustainable performance. *Sustainability, 14*(14), 8737. https://doi.org/10.3390/su14148737

Yeshua-Katz, D., & Efrat-Treister, D. (2021). 'Together in the tech trenches': A view of Israel's innovation culture. *Innovation, 23*(3), 337–353. https://doi.org/10.1080/14479338.2020.1758565

Yi-Ru, R.C., Chun-Ju, F.H-.B., & Xianhong, C. (2020). Moving forward the dialogic theory of public relations: Concepts, methods and applications of organization-public dialogue. *Public Relations Review, 46*(1), 1–6. https://doi.org/10.1016/j.pubrev.2019.101878

4 On organizational listening

Subtextual organizational listening to sounds of silence

Ganga S. Dhanesh

Abstract

This chapter explores the impact of cultural factors on the practice of organizational listening in the United Arab Emirates (UAE). Specifically, it explores how aspects of an economically vibrant federation amidst a geopolitical tinderbox in the Middle East, characterized by high-context, indirect, oral cultures in a melting pot of over 200 nationalities, a highly calibrated media system, and limited appetite for activism can affect the enactment of organizational listening. How does the idea of listening as proposed in the assertive, literate cultures of the West fit the associative, oral cultures of the Arab world? In response, this chapter proposes the concept of *subtextual organizational listening*. Defined as organizational listening where communication is indirect and nuanced, often relying on unspoken or implied messages rather than overt speech, *subtextual organizational listening* reflects the idea of listening to what is not directly said, but is understood through context, tone, gestures, or shared knowledge, needed in high-context cultures with restrictions on free speech. This chapter illustrates how the concept of *subtextual organizational listening* could have improved outcomes in the case of the Starbucks consumer boycott over the Gaza war.

Organizational listening

Public relations has been defined as the strategic use of communication to foster relationships between organizations and their various publics. This concept of strategic communication is largely grounded

DOI: 10.4324/9781003368366-4

in the normative idea of two-way communication flows between organizations and their audiences (Grunig, 2001; Kent & Taylor, 2002; Taylor & Kent, 2014). The dialogic theory of public relations further emphasizes that true dialogue is essential for building meaningful relationships between organizations and their publics (Kent & Taylor, 2002). Thus, public relations practitioners are considered boundary spanners between organizations and various publics who facilitate the flow of information around specific issues, organizations, and publics. Although two-way communication flows, symmetrical communication, and a dialogic orientation to relationship building implies both speaking and listening, scholars have criticized public relations research and practice for not giving enough attention to organizational listening (Macnamara, 2018; 2023). Macnamara (2016) argued that organizations have engaged in an *architecture of speaking* disregarding an *architecture of listening* (p. 162), leading to a *crisis of listening* (p. 156).

Macnamara (2016) reported on The Organizational Listening Project, which examined how 36 organizations from the corporate, government, and nongovernment sectors in Australia, the UK, and the USA listened to their stakeholders. These stakeholders included employees, shareholders, customers, and other constituents, such as members, patients, students, and local communities. The findings revealed that most organizational communication focused overwhelmingly on speaking rather than listening, with many organizations performing poorly in listening to their stakeholders.

Through his work, Macnamara (e.g., 2016, 2018, 2023) developed a theory of organizational listening within public relations, identifying seven canons of effective listening: giving recognition to others, acknowledgment of others' views, paying attention to others, interpreting what others say, understanding others views and perspectives, considering what others say, and responding in an appropriate way. Further, Macnamara offered an *architecture of listening* that involves building an organizational culture that values listening, establishing policies that encourage listening practices, addressing the power dynamics involved in listening (referred to as the politics of listening), and creating systems to facilitate listening. Additionally, this architecture emphasizes the importance of utilizing suitable listening technologies, allocating adequate resources, fostering listening skills, and integrating listening into decision-making and policy-making processes. Other factors identified as important characteristics of listening include being open, active or even proactive, reciprocal, and ideally mindful and empathetic (Macnamara, 2016; 2018).

Additionally, Macnamara (2023) emphasized that the organizational listening being promoted is a form of ethical listening, integral to fostering engagement and dialogue between organizations and their stakeholders. This type of listening is crucial for genuine communication to take place; without it, communication devolves into a monologue that not only leads to silence from others but may also actively suppress their voices. The notion of ethical listening distinguishes it from and draws clear bounds around espionage for national security that can impinge on privacy and human rights, and unethical corporate practices of social media surveillance for targeting stakeholders.

Ethical organizational listening is seen as crucial from a strategic perspective (Lewis, 2020; Macnamara, 2023; Reinikainen et al., 2020) that can lead to increased employee engagement, customer loyalty, organizational legitimacy, and mitigate crises (Fu & Wang, 2024; Neill & Bowen, 2021; Men et al., 2022). It can also help to navigate organizational change by being a key mediating factor between organizational identity and effective organizational change (Fu et al., 2024). It can contribute to fostering civic engagement (Canel, 2022; Capizzo & Feinman, 2022; Capizzo & Sommerfeldt, 2023) and social equity through listening that addresses intersectionality (Place, 2022), and across cultures (Bachman & Labarca, 2023).

However, companies have often been criticized for not engaging in true listening but engaging in *pseudo listening* or *inauthentic listening* (Macnamara, 2018; 2023; Sahay, 2021; Tam et al., 2023). Companies usually speak unilaterally and do not listen. Even if they do and engage in two-way communication, it is with the asymmetric intention of gaining audience insights to influence audiences, benefiting the company. Listening with empathy and listening with the intention to accept responsibility and change is limited (Macnamara, 2018; Sahay, 2021; Tam et al., 2023).

Beyond these criticisms of the literature on poor organizational listening, this chapter argues that the concept of listening itself is rooted in Western values, particularly the underpinning ideologies of individualism, democracy, voice, freedom of speech, marketization, consumption, and self-promotion, which might not automatically transfer to non-Western contexts (Edwards, 2018; Valentini et al., 2016; Zaharna, 2016). As Macnamara (2016) had argued, every communicative situation involves speaking and listening. But what if there are scarce sounds to listen to? In nondemocratic contexts with limitations on free speech, where there are restrictions on what can be aired in public, what if there are no stakeholder voices to listen to? How can organizations listen when faced with sounds of silence? This chapter argues that diverse political, economic, societal, and media cultures can affect the occurrence and practice of organizational listening. However, there is limited research on the impact of diverse cultural contexts on the practice of organizational listening.

Although Macnamara (2023) highlighted the need to listen across cultures, limited research has focused on the impact of diverse cultural contexts on the conceptualization and implementation of organizational listening. Place's (2023) edited book *Organizational Listening for Strategic Communication* has a final section titled, "Cultural and Global Considerations for Organizational Listening," which includes two chapters. One chapter discussed the need to extend listening research to international contexts and offered an example of Latin America, where the authors argued that the practice and analysis of organizational listening must be examined within a web of socio-political factors such as distrust based on a history of colonialism, political instability, human rights violations, and social inequalities (Bachman & Labarca, 2023). The other chapter highlighted the need for listening across borders in the case of public diplomacy (Storie & Marschlich, 2023).

Building on a similar argument as Bachman and Labarca (2023), this chapter considers how varied cultural factors could affect the practice of organizational listening in the United Arab Emirates (UAE). Specifically, we define culture broadly as encompassing political, economic, societal, media, and activism cultures as articulated within the global public relations framework (GPRF) (Sriramesh & Vercic, 2009; 2019). Within the general macro variables of the GPRF, we will examine micro-cultural variables specific to the context of the UAE that could influence listening as a public relations concept situated within local and global contexts of practice because culture-general and culture-specific studies complement each other to provide a more holistic culturally grounded view of local practices situated in a globally interconnected world (Zaharna, 2022).

Cultural factors and organizational listening in the UAE

This chapter will focus on the characteristics of the UAE political system, societal culture, media, and activism. However, it is important to keep in mind that although this chapter addresses only four cultural factors, the five factors in the GPRF are interconnected, thereby influencing and being influenced by one another.

Political system: An oasis in a tinderbox of geopolitical tensions

The political system of a nation-state significantly impacts the lives of its individuals, publics, and organizations. The UAE is described as a constitutional federation of seven emirates located in the eastern part of the Arabian Peninsula comprising Abu Dhabi, Dubai, Sharjah, Ajman, Umm Al Quwain, Ras Al Khaimah, and Fujairah. The federation, established in 1971, is run by a federal government and local governments of the seven emirates. The President, elected by the Federal Supreme Council, serves as the head of state, with executive power shared among the hereditary rulers of the individual emirates. Abu Dhabi, the largest emirate, is the capital of the UAE. The country is part of the Gulf Cooperation Council (GCC), a regional, political, and economic entity comprising Bahrain, Kuwait, Oman, Qatar, Saudi Arabia, and the UAE (UAE Government Portal, n.d., a).

According to the 2023 Democracy Index from the Economist Intelligence Unit, which evaluates 167 countries and classifies them into four types of regimes—full democracy, flawed democracy, hybrid regime, and authoritarian regime—the Middle East and North Africa ranked lowest, largely due to the impact of the Israel-Hamas war. However, the UAE was the only country in the region to improve its score. This improvement resulted from a boost in the country's political participation score, driven by a rise in the representation of women in the Federal National Council (FNC) in the October 2023 election, following the adoption of a directive passed in 2019 mandating that women represent 50% of the 20 candidates elected in the 40-member Council (EIU, 2024).

While the EIU Democracy Index 2023 has listed the UAE as an authoritarian regime (EIU, 2024), others have noted that although "traditionally conservative and authoritarian in government, the UAE is one of the most liberal countries in the Gulf, with other cultures and beliefs generally tolerated" (BBC, 2023). Indeed, for the 12th consecutive year, Arab youth has ranked the UAE as the country they would like most to live in, and as the aspirational country Arab youth want their own country to be like (AsdaaBCW, 2023).

Pertinent aspects of the political system that could potentially influence organizational listening include the country's long-standing history with the tinderbox of regional politics, particularly the tension between diverse modes of governance and its impact on public opinion and freedom of expression. "Ideological contests in the MENA region between secular authoritarian models of governance and political Islamist ones continue, though space for freedom of expression has been closed in almost every state in the region" (Vakil & Quilliam, 2023, p. 8). In response to the widespread uprisings across much of the Arab world in 2011, the UAE had proactively strengthened its control over political expression within the country. In 2012, the UAE intensified its efforts to curb dissent by enacting new laws that prohibited public or online criticism of the government. However, the UAE had also taken steps to enhance civic engagement among its own citizens. Since 2006, 20 members of the FNC have been elected by an electoral college, and 20 are nominated by the rulers of the respective emirates. This electoral college had been broadened to encompass approximately one-third of the voting-age population by 2015 (Britannica, 2024). Further, the UAE was also not impacted much by the uprisings across the Middle East because of the high quality of life and economic opportunities it offered to its citizens (CIA World Factbook, 2024). Arab youth appeared to appreciate this fine balance between free expression, political stability, and economic vibrancy. While 46% of Arab youth across the Middle East—including GCC, North Africa and the Levant—said that their voice does not matter to their country's leadership, 78% of youth in the GCC, which includes the UAE, said otherwise (AsdaaBCW, 2023). They also appreciated the UAE for being safe, for its growing economy, and effective and visionary leadership (AsdaaBCW, 2023).

After the Arab uprisings of 2011, the UAE also began to take a more active role in regional affairs, playing a major role in the regional crackdown on the Muslim Brotherhood, an Islamist religio-political organization, and its related entities. The UAE also participated in the 2017–21 blockade of Qatar, seen as an attempt to stave off influence from both the Muslim Brotherhood and Iran in the region. More recently, the UAE signed the Abraham Accords in August 2020, normalizing relations with Israel, and becoming the first Gulf Arab country to do so (Peterson & Crystal, 2024). These political moves were aimed at boosting the UAE's soft power, as envisioned in The UAE Soft Power Strategy (UAE Government, n.d., b).

According to the GPRF, strategic public relations practices thrive on public opinion, which tends to flourish in pluralistic societies typically associated with democracies (Sriramesh & Vercic, 2009; 2019). If public opinion does not flourish in nondemocratic contexts, then what does that mean for organizational listening? Due to a confluence of factors mentioned above, such as maintaining peace and security for an economically vibrant society, which has a per capita GDP on par with Western European nations (CIA World Factbook, 2024), there are restrictions on political expression, especially criticism of the government, leading to an apparent vacuum of publics' voices. This is also compounded by the predominantly expatriate population (88%) of the country, who are not citizens (UAE Ministry of Foreign Affairs, n.d.).

Societal culture: High context, indirect, oral cultures in a melting pot of diversity

The GPRF argued that if culture affects communication and vice versa, and if public relations is predicated on communication, then culture should affect public relations and vice versa (Sriramesh & Vercic, 2009; 2019). The cultural diversity of the Middle East in terms of ethnicity, religion, and language is even more pronounced in the UAE, which has a predominantly expatriate population. Indians form the largest foreign community in the UAE, followed by Pakistanis, Bangladeshis, other Asians, Europeans, and Africans (UAE Ministry of Foreign Affairs). While the population is made up of 200 different nationalities and many faiths, with 74.5% Muslims, Islam is the official religion in the UAE (CIA World Factbook, 2024). However, with a veritable melting pot of nationalities who live and work together, the UAE government foregrounds values of inclusion and tolerance, hosting more than 40 churches, two Hindu temples, a Sikh temple, and a Buddhist temple, which welcome multinational congregations (UAE Embassy, n.d.).

Situated within the Arabian Peninsula, the UAE's societal culture reflects traditional Arab and Islamic values. Al-Kandari and Gaither (2011) employed the cultural-economic model of international public relations and identified cultural value orientations that influence Arab culture, such as commitment to religion, devotion to the group, resistance to change/attachment to history, and recognition of hierarchal order. Some of the distinct features of the UAE's cultural fabric are tolerance, family cohesion, and solidarity among members of the society. Strong clan/tribe affiliations continue to exist as everyone belonged to a tribal group to which they swore allegiance (UAE Government Portal, n.d., c)

In Arab communication patterns, the role of the listener is pivotal due to the cultural emphasis on relationships and social context. Zaharna (2010) highlighted that intercultural competence in the Arab world centers around understanding the importance of relationships rather than just the direct transmission of information. This perspective is rooted in what Zaharna called the "associative" perspective, closely aligned with Hall's (1976) concept of "high-context" cultures. In these cultures, much of the meaning is implied in the context rather than stated explicitly through words, placing a significant interpretive responsibility on the listener.

In high-context communication, speakers expect listeners to intuitively grasp what is left unsaid. As Hall (1976) explained, a high-context individual will often arrange details without directly revealing the main idea. The effectiveness of this subtle exchange relies on the listener's ability to decode unspoken cues embedded in the relationship between speaker and audience. As Zaharna (1995) noted, the onus for comprehension lies not with the speaker but with the listener's skill in interpreting context. This dynamic is also seen in public relations and communication strategies in the Arab world, where understanding meaning often requires "contexting" and "indirectness." Practitioners must be aware that Arab listeners may treat certain details as self-evident, relying heavily on relational clues. Zaharna (2010) described this as relational communication, emphasizing that effective listening involves an attunement to social dynamics rather than merely processing information.

Further, Arab cultures tend to be oral cultures, wherein listeners are deeply involved in constructing meaning, going to great lengths to make sense of the speaker's message. Unlike literate cultures that focus on factual accuracy and the written word, oral cultures often value the emotional resonance of a message. Tannen (1982) observed that speakers in these settings aim to evoke an emotional, participatory response, with the listener actively collaborating in the communicative process. In this context, the listener is not a passive recipient but an active co-creator of meaning, interpreting through relational cues and cultural understanding rather than direct information.

Although the UAE might represent multiple aspects of Arab culture, such as relational communication, where the burden of understanding meaning falls on the listener, it is also a country that aims to become a global player with a strong foreign direct investment orientation, attracting global players in finance, banking, trade, and investment sectors. What could a melting pot of communication patterns with a predominant slant toward relational communication mean for organizational listening? Public relations practitioners might have to employ a plethora of communication strategies, including mediated and face-to-face communication that might help them to be active listeners, who can grasp meanings that are embedded in contexts and emotions.

Media: Calibrated expression

The GPRF acknowledged the power of mass media to influence public opinion and shape public discourse, hence holding significant influence over organizational activities in general and public relations in particular. However, as per the GPRF, media relations will be dependent on the extent of media control, media diffusion, and media access (Sriramesh & Vercic, 2009; 2019).

In the UAE, the majority of domestic media outlets are owned and operated by the state-owned Abu Dhabi Media and Dubai Media Incorporated, with the country's media outlets governed by government-owned organizations, as well as the National Media Council and related entities. While the country's constitution guarantees freedom of expression, under a 1980 federal law, the authorities can censor media content deemed to be excessively critical of policies, the ruling families, religion, or the economy (Reporters Without Borders, n.d.). The Federal Decree-Law No. 55 of 2023 regulates media activities in the UAE, encompassing various formats like broadcasting, publications, and digital media. It permits both individuals and entities to own media outlets under specific conditions and sets national standards for content, emphasizing respect for religious beliefs, national values, and privacy. Violations may result in fines, closures, or license cancellations (UAE Government Portal, n.d., d). Prohibited media content includes offenses against Islam, or anything else that could jeopardize the UAE's larger interests; opinions that violate public morals, or advocates for the adoption of damaging ideas; and any false accusations of Arabs or anything that misrepresents their civilization or tradition (UAE Government Portal, n.d., d). Freedom House ranks the UAE as not free with a score of 18/100 (Freedom House, 2024).

As for media diffusion or reach, it is noteworthy that social media penetration in the UAE has achieved a high of 115% (Dixon, 2024). Social network websites remained the top source of news for more than half of UAE (52%), followed by television, newspapers' websites, and news apps on a mobile or tablet device in 2023, with 55% of the population preferring to read news content online than in print newspapers. Top newspaper apps visited included Khaleej Times, Gulf News, BBC, The National, and Emirates247 (Shah, 2024). The country's leading daily in terms of circulation is Al-Khaleej, published in the emirate of Sharjah, while the oldest is Al-Ittihad, which is financed by the Abu Dhabi Media group. English-language dailies, such as Gulf News and The National, are also very influential (Reporters Without Borders, n.d.)

While organizations have direct access to the media, consistent with the prevalence of the personal influence model in the region, some of the commonly used models of media relations including press agentry, and one-way, asymmetrical, public information models highlight the purpose of public relations—to gain publicity and enhance the image of the organization (Al-Kindi, 2019; Kirat, 2015; Zayani, 2008). However, a culture-centered model of communication in the UAE that can be regarded as two-way could be the *majlis*, employed as an informal participatory public forum for men in enabling direct access to the rulers in a political system that is tradition-based and patriarchal (Badran, 2019; Badran et al., 2003).

Despite restrictions on freedom of the press, UAE residents' trust in news organizations that have a reputation for objectivity, proven by track record, has improved (Shah, 2024). However, Storie (2015) found that cultural and linguistic proximity, and the perceived risks and dangers of online engagement due to laws and internal political climate, predicted young adult publics' preferences for online engagement, which could directly influence the robustness of the public sphere and hence relative silence in mediated spaces that could have implications for organizational listening.

Activism: What activism?

According to the GPRF, a country's political system has a direct influence on the level of activism in the country because only economically developed, pluralistic societies tend to foster activism (Sriramesh & Vercic, 2009; 2019). The UAE does not have a history of traditional activism. In many Arab states, certain stakeholder groups, such as trade unions and lobbyists, are generally disfavored (Ararat, 2006). The establishment of employees' representatives, trade unions, and workers' councils and committees is not provided for under any of the laws of the UAE (Howse, 2024).

Although the Arab Spring tore through multiple countries in the Middle East and North Africa over 2010 and 2011, the UAE did not experience the unrest seen elsewhere, partly because of the government's multi-year, billion-dollar infrastructure investment plan for the economically less advanced northern emirates, and its active control of advocates for political reform (CIA World Factbook, 2024). More recently, the UAE arrested and later pardoned 57 Bangladeshis who were sentenced to long prison terms for staging protests in the UAE against their own government in Bangladesh. The protesters had been charged with gathering in a public place with the aim of inciting unrest (Comerford, 2024).

However, as part of the conditions for hosting COP28, the climate change conference, the UAE had agreed to permit protests in accordance with U.N. guidelines, which require prior approval for any demonstrations and restrict them to the summit site. A small group of demonstrators demanded the release of pro-democracy activists imprisoned in the UAE and Egypt, with most protests occurring within the summit's "blue zone," an area under U.N. control where local laws do not apply (Reuters, 2023). Outside the contexts of political protest and conflict, Allagui (2017) explored the influence of corporate public relations activism in monarchical settings and found that public relations practitioners and senior managers were actively engaged in social activism via corporate campaigns.

In short, while the UAE shares many characteristics with neighboring countries in the MENA region, particularly in terms of political systems and cultural traditions, its record of political stability, economic growth, social tolerance and inclusion, a highly calibrated media, and limited appetite for activism distinguishes it from others, highlighting its unique attributes that dialectically straddle multiple opposing tensions. I next propose an approach to organizational listening in such a context.

Organizational listening in a calibrated, high context, indirect, oral culture: Proposing subtextual organizational listening

The description of the UAE, as per its political, societal, media, and activist cultures, has revealed a complicated context, rife with dialectical tensions that could affect organizational listening. For multiple reasons that could potentially include maintaining peace and economic vibrancy in a region simmering with wars, conflicts, and geopolitical tensions, there are restrictions on what can be publicly shared, including on social media. Furthermore, although the UAE's societal culture reflects multiple aspects of Arab culture, such as relational communication, it is also a country that hosts 200 nationalities and attracts global foreign players in finance, banking, etc., which underscores the need to straddle local and global modes of effective communication.

This chapter argues that the concept of organizational listening is particularly suited for oral cultures, such as the Arab culture, because it is closely connected to speaking. In oral cultures, communication relies on both listening and speaking, unlike literate cultures where the written word reigns. Not surprisingly, in public relations literature, predominantly generated from the literate cultures of the USA and Western Europe, public relations tactics and tools are primarily focused on the written word in news releases, websites, social media posts, speeches, and blogs. The attention paid to visual and oral communication is rather limited. However, for an oral culture, the idea of listening is a perfectly natural fit.

How does the idea of listening as proposed in the assertive, literate cultures of the West fit the associative, oral cultures of the Arab world? The elements of organizational listening include an organizational culture of listening, establishing policies that encourage listening, paying attention to the politics of listening, instituting systems of listening, organizing listening technologies, marshaling resources, ensuring appropriate skills, and directing insights from listening to influence decision and policy-making (Macnamara, 2016; 2018; 2023). While all of these are important in the oral cultures of the Arab world, probably what takes on greater prominence are the elements of addressing politics, instituting listening technologies, and ensuring appropriate skills.

First, addressing politics does not necessarily refer to inequities among the relational entities but could refer to the broader social and political contexts in which the listening occurs. Organizations must be cognizant of the political contexts in which organizational listening occurs. If the contexts are navigating tricky areas of peace versus volatility when located within a broader region of geopolitical tension, then it could have repercussions on what can be listened to.

Second, while listening technologies typically refer to mediated technologies such as social media, websites, or blogs, in predominantly oral cultures compounded by media laws that restrict the extent of free speech online and offline, it might be more effective to employ face-to-face listening technologies. Face-to-face listening also leverages the personal influence model prevalent in the UAE, as well as the assertion of public relations leaders in the Middle East that Middle Eastern cultures prize the personal touch (Derrick, 2023).

Third, ensuring an organization's listening skills and competencies should include the ability to read high-context communication, where messages are embedded more in the context than in the code. It should include the ability to read emotional themes in the messaging because the onus of understanding meaning and context lies on the organizational listener. Hence, the seven canons of listening take on additional importance in oral cultures, which place an ordinate responsibility on the listener, in this case, the organization. This could be referred to as high-context, subtextual, aural listening for meaning embedded in the context; listening for emotional valence and imagery. This is listening to *vox populi*, but it is not *vox populi* which has similar connotations in literate cultures that are more direct and low context. This is listening in a high-context oral culture with indirect communication patterns, or *subtextual listening*.

Subtextual organizational listening is defined as organizational listening where communication is indirect and nuanced, often relying on unspoken or implied messages rather than overt speech. In high-context cultures with restrictions on free speech, the ability to read between the lines and interpret subtle cues becomes a crucial aspect of organizational listening. It captures the idea of listening to what is not directly said, but is understood through context, tone, gestures, or shared knowledge.

To summarize, a culture-general theoretical framework such as the GPRF has shown that the political, societal, media, and activist cultures can influence the practice of public relations in specific contexts, influenced by specific cultural factors that might be unique to the situation. In the case of the UAE, specifics include a delicate political situation wherein the UAE maintains peace and prosperity internally while navigating a tinderbox of regional volatility through exerting soft power in the region; a societal culture that values relational communication with deep emotional resonance in an oral society where the "burden of meaning" is on the listener; carefully calibrated control over free expression that is compounded by laws that prohibit free speech; and traditionally low tolerance for activism, being deliberately calibrated as the country seeks global prominence. All of these factors gently nudge the enactment of organizational listening towards the form of *subtextual organizational listening*. The next section discusses a case study that illustrates the boundaries of the generic concept of organizational listening and highlights the potential of *subtextual organizational listening*.

Case study: Starbucks and consumer boycott over the Gaza war in the UAE

Following the Gaza war outbreak on October 7, 2023, Starbucks faced a significant backlash, especially in the UAE and the Middle East, due to allegations of supporting Israel financially. The crisis began in the USA on October 9, 2023, when Starbucks Workers United, a U.S.-based union, posted "Solidarity with Palestine" on the social media platform X. The unauthorized post was quickly deleted but sparked calls for a Starbucks boycott, especially among pro-Israel supporters in the USA. In response, Starbucks publicly distanced itself, issuing a statement on October 13 condemning violence and disavowing the union's message. This incident led to a legal tussle between Starbucks USA and the union, with both parties suing each other over the use of the brand name and logo. Starbucks faced backlash from both pro-Palestinian and pro-Israel groups, affecting its reputation and resulting in store vandalism. Starbucks CEO Laxman Narasimhan cited "mis-representation on social media" as a factor fueling protests and reiterated the company's neutral stance, condemning all forms of hate and violence. This incident attracted widespread media attention, with Starbucks USA reporting that the union's actions on X had angered many customers domestically, damaging the company's reputation (Rennolds, 2024). The company further claimed that some protests and calls to boycott Starbucks were directly fueled by the union's comments (Meyersohn, 2023).

Although the boycotts began in the United States, they quickly spread to other regions, particularly the Middle East, highlighting the interconnectedness of the global economy. In this region, the Kuwait-based Alshaya Group, a major retail player in the Middle East and North Africa (MENA), operates Starbucks exclusively. With approximately 1,900 Starbucks outlets and close to 70 consumer retail brands across Turkey, MENA, and Europe, Alshaya wields substantial influence in the region's food and beverage industry. However, by January 2024, Alshaya Group reported that the boycotts had negatively impacted their business, causing them to miss their Q1 revenue expectations. The company estimated losses of $11 billion, as recorded in December 2023 (Fast Company Middle East, 2024).

Meanwhile, the hashtag "boycott Starbucks" gained traction on social media across the Middle East, with consumers sharing videos encouraging followers to choose alternative coffee options. Videos showing empty Starbucks stores circulated widely, reflecting the boycott's impact. In a country that has limited tolerance for traditional activism, hashtag activism that spanned national borders gained support and targeted an international iconic brand that purportedly supported the genocide in Palestine. The void of traditional activism was being filled by hashtag activism that translated into behavioral activism through customer boycott.

In a bid to demonstrate solidarity with Gaza, Starbucks UAE launched a campaign on April 16, 2024, under the hashtag #WeStandForHumanity on its Instagram account. This campaign reiterated Starbucks' global position on the issue, highlighting the Starbucks Foundation and Alshaya Group's pledge to provide one million meals to families in Gaza, in collaboration with World Central Kitchen. The campaign was widely promoted on the company's website and social media platforms. Starbucks UAE also introduced a Q&A page to address consumer inquiries regarding whether Starbucks or Howard Schultz, the former chairman, president, and CEO of Starbucks, had provided financial support to Israel or the Israeli government. All of these one-way communication strategies foregrounded the organization's *architecture of speaking*.

These efforts at corporate speaking proved insufficient in mitigating the boycott's impact. The boycotts persisted, underscoring the ongoing challenges Starbucks and Alshaya Group face in attempting to reconcile the brand's perceived stance with public sentiment across diverse global markets. On March 6, 2024, Alshaya Group announced job cuts in its Starbucks franchises across the MENA region, affecting approximately 4% of its 50,000-strong workforce (Al Sayegh, 2024).

An architecture of *subtextual organizational listening*, adapted to the political, societal, media, and activist cultures of the country, could have alerted Starbucks well in advance. First, if Starbucks had considered its global presence as an iconic American brand with a founder of Jewish heritage, it could have responded to the initial tweet with far more intercultural sensitivity. Second, its architecture of listening could have been cognizant of the political context of the country, which exerted considerable influence on what could be shared online by local publics. Hence, they could have engaged more with models of personal influence and employed nonmediated forms of listening that could have grasped the underlying emotional charge of the issue for the Arab population in the UAE.. This could have delivered the personal touch that is valued in Middle Eastern cultures. Engaging in high-context *subtextual organizational listening* could have alerted them to meanings embedded in the contexts and not the code. Most importantly, by aligning organizational listening with the cultures of the country, Starbucks UAE might have had a fighting chance to distance itself from the home brand and highlight its connections to the local franchisee and rein in the damage to the brand locally.

Questions for further discussion

1 How can a combination of macro and micro cultural factors affect organizational listening?
2 Do you think multinational companies face additional challenges in creating architectures of listening when compared to local companies?
3 How can architectures of organizational listening be designed for multinational organizations that operate in different countries?
4 Can you think of another example where organizational listening, attuned to or not attuned to cultural factors, had a deep impact on the organization?
5 Will these cultural factors affect companies in the public, private, and NGO sectors?

References

Al-Kandari, A., & Gaither, T.K. (2011). Arabs, the west and public relations: A critical/cultural study of Arab cultural values. *Public Relations Review, 37*(3), 266–273. https://doi.org/10.1016/j.pubrev.2011.04.002

Al-Kindi, A.K. (2019). Public relations units in the Omani civil service sector: Historical background and current characteristics. In T.M. Almutairi and D. Kruckeberg (Eds.). *Public Relations in the Gulf Cooperation Countries: An Arab Perspective*, pp. 53–73. Routledge. https://doi.org/10.4324/9781351064989-4

Allagui, I. (2017). Towards organizational activism in the UAE: A case study approach. *Public Relations Review*, *43*, 258–266. https://doi.org/10.1016/j.pubrev.2016.12.007

AlSayegh, H. (2024, March 5). Exclusive: Starbucks Middle East franchisee AlShaya to cut over 2,000 jobs, sources say. *Reuters*. www.reuters.com/business/retail-consumer/starbucks-middle-east-franchisee-alshaya-cut-over-2000-jobs-sources-say-2024-03-05/

Ararat, M. (2006, April 1). *Corporate social responsibility across Middle East and North Africa*. http://ssrn.com/abstract=1015925

AsdaaBCW (2023). *Arab Youth Survey – Living a new reality*. https://arabyouthsurvey.com/en/

Bachman, I., & Labarca, C. (2023). The local and the global in organizational listening amid an evolving media landscape. In K.R. Place (Ed.). *Organizational Listening for Strategic Communication: Building Theory and Practice*. Routledge. https://doi.org/10.4324/9781003273851-19

Badran, B., Turk, J., & Walters, T. (2003). Sharing the transformation: Public relations and the UAE come of age. In K. Sriramesh and D. Vercic (Eds.). *The Global Public Relations Handbook Theory, Research and Practice*, pp. 46–67. Routledge.

Badran, B.A. (2019). A critical snapshot of the practice of public relations in the United Arab Emirates. In T.M. Almutairi and D. Kruckeberg (Eds.). *Public Relations in the Gulf Cooperation Countries: An Arab Perspective*, pp. 118–144. Routledge. https://doi.org/10.4324/9781351064989-7

BBC (2023, September 7). *United Arab Emirates Country Profile*. www.bbc.com/news/world-middle-east-14703998

Britannica (2024, November 5). UAE – Foreign Relations. www.britannica.com/place/United-Arab-Emirates/Foreign-relations

Canel, M.J., Barandiarán, X., & Murphy, A. (2022). What does learning by listening bring to citizen engagement? Lessons from a government program. Public Relations Review, 48(1), 102132. https://doi.org/10.1016/j.pubrev.2021.102132

Capizzo, L., & Feinman, M. (2022). Extending civic values in architectures of listening: Arendt, Mouffe and the pluralistic imperative for organizational listening. *Journal of Public Relations Research, 34*(6), 274–295. https://doi.org/10.1080/1062726X.2022.2127728

Capizzo, L., & Sommerfeldt, E.J. (2023). Cultivating listening spaces for civil society: Reorienting public relations amid Hannah Arendt's urgent pluralism. *Public Relations Review, 49*(4), 102351. https://doi.org/10.1016/j.pubrev.2023.102351

CIA World Factbook (2024). *United Arab Emirates: Middle East*. www.cia.gov/the-world-factbook/countries/united-arab-emirates/

Comerford, R. (2024, September 3). UAE pardons Bangladeshis jailed for protesting. *BBC*. www.bbc.com/news/articles/cx2l127dr9jo

Derrick, S. (2023, October 16). Redefining PR in the Middle East: Strategies, growth, and culture. *PR Week*. www.prweek.com/article/1838953/redefining-pr-middle-east.

Dixon, S.J. (2024). Social media: Active usage penetration in selected countries and territories 2024. *Statista*. www.statista.com/statistics/282846/regular-social-networking-usage-penetration-worldwide-by-country/

Edwards, L. (2018). *Public relations and globalisation. Understanding public relations: Theory, culture and society (ch.7)*. SAGE Publications. https://doi.org/10.4135/9781473983571

EIU (2024, February 15). *Democracy index: Conflict and polarisation drive a new low for global democracy*. www.eiu.com/n/democracy-index-conflict-and-polarisation-drive-a-new-low-for-global-democracy/

Fast Company Middle East (2024, June 3). *Starbucks Middle East stores to lay off 2000 amid boycott calls over Gaza war*. https://fastcompanyme.com/news/starbucks-middle-east-stores-to-lay-off-2000-amid-boycott-calls-over-gaza-war/

Freedom House (2024). *Freedom in the world 2024 – United Arab Emirates*. https://freedomhouse.org/country/united-arab-emirates/freedom-world/2024

Fu, J.S., & Wang, R. (2024). Multiple pathways to organizational legitimacy: Information visibility, organizational listening, and cross-sector partnerships. *Public Relations Review*, *50*(4). https://doi.org/10.1016/j.pubrev.2024.102484

Fu, J.S., Woo, D., Cooper, K.R., & Kwestel, M. (2024). Navigating multiple identities for positive change through organizational listening. *Communication Research*. https://doi.org/10.1177/00936502241227380

Grunig, J.E. (2001). Two-way symmetrical public relations: Past, present, and future. In R. L. Heath (Ed.). Handbook of Public Relations (pp. 11–30). Sage. https://doi.org/10.4135/9781452220727.n1

Hall, E.T. (1976). *Beyond culture*. New York, NY: Anchor.

Howse, M. (2024). *Labour & Employment 2024: United Arab Emirates*. Morgan Lewis. www.morganlewis.com/pubs/2024/07/gtdt-2024-uae

Kent, M.L., & Taylor, M. (2002). Toward a dialogic theory of public relations. *Public Relations Review, 28*(1), 21–37. https://doi.org/10.1016/S0363-8111(02)00108-X

Kirat, M. (2015). Corporate social responsibility in the oil and gas industry in Qatar: Perceptions and practices. *Public Relations Review, 41*(4), 438–446. https://doi.org/10.1016/j.pubrev.2015.07.001

Lewis, L.K. (2020). *The power of strategic listening*. Rowman & Littlefield Publishers.

Macnamara, J. (2016). Organizational listening: Addressing a major gap in public relations theory and practice. *Journal of Public Relations Research, 28*(3-4), 146–169. https://doi.org/10.1080/1062726X.2016.1228064

Macnamara, J. (2018). Toward a theory and practice of organizational listening. *International Journal of Listening, 32*(1), 1–23. https://doi.org/10.1080/10904018.2017.1375076

Macnamara, J. (2023). *Organizational listening II: Expanding the concept, theory, and practice* (2nd Edition). Peter Lang.

Men, L.R., Zhou, A., & Tsai, W.S. (2022). Harnessing the power of chatbot social conversation for organizational listening: The impact on perceived transparency and organization-public relationships. *Journal of Public Relations Research, 34*(1–2), 20–44. https://doi.org/10.1080/1062726X.2022.2068553

Meyersohn, N. (2023, December 21). Starbucks' CEO wants people to stop protesting its stores over Israel war in Gaza. *CNN Business*. https://edition.cnn.com/2023/12/21/business/starbucks-israel-war-union/index.html

Neill, M.S., & Bowen, S.A. (2021). Employee perceptions of ethical listening in US organizations. *Public Relations Review, 47*(5), 102123. https://doi.org/10.1016/j.pubrev.2021.102123

Peterson, J.E., & Crystal, J.A. (2024, September 29). *Foreign Relations*. Britannica. www.britannica.com/place/United-Arab-Emirates/Foreign-relations

Place, K.R. (2022). Toward a framework for listening with consideration for intersectionality: Insights from public relations professionals in borderland spaces. *Journal of Public Relations Research, 34*(1–2), 4–19. https://doi.org/10.1080/1062726X.2022.2057502

Place, K.R. (2023). *Organizational listening for strategic communication building theory and practice*. Routledge. https://doi.org/10.4324/9781003273851

Reinikainen, H., Kari, J., & Luoma-aho, V. (2020). Generation Z and organizational listening on social media. *Media and Communication, 8*(2), 185–196. https://doi.org/10.17645/mac.v8i2.2772

Rennolds, N. (2024, March 9). Starbucks Middle East franchisee to slash over 2,000 jobs as boycotts linked to the Israel-Gaza conflict hit Western brands, says report. *Business Insider*. www.businessinsider.com/starbucks-middle-east-franchisee-slash-jobs

Reporters Without Borders (n.d.). *United Arab Emirates*. https://rsf.org/en/country/united-arab-emirates

Reuters (2023, December 9). *Activists stage rare UAE politics protest during COP28 climate summit*. www.reuters.com/world/middle-east/activists-stage-rare-uae-politics-protest-during-cop28-climate-summit-2023-12-09/

Sahay, S. (2021). Organizational listening during organizational change: Perspectives of employees and executives. *International Journal of Listening, 37*(1), 12–25. https://doi.org/10.1080/10904018.2021.1941029

Shah, S. (2024). *The UAE Media Morph – 2024 trend report*. YouGov. https://business.yougov.com/content/48808-the-uae-media-morph-2024-trend-report

Sriramesh, K., & Vercic, D. (2009). A theoretical framework for global public relations research and practice. In K. Sriramesh and D. Vercic (Eds.). *The Global Public Relations Handbook: Theory, Research and Practice* (2nd Edition), pp. 3–21. Routledge. https://doi.org/10.4324/9780203889374

Sriramesh, K., & Vercic, D. (2019). *The global public relations handbook: Theory, research and practice* (3rd Edition). Routledge. https://doi.org/10.4324/9781315173290

Storie, L.K. (2015). Lost publics in public diplomacy: Antecedents for online relationship management. *Public Relations Review, 41*(2), 315–317. https://doi.org/10.1016/j.pubrev.2015.02.008

Storie, L.K., & Marschlich, S. (2023). Listening across borders: Global considerations for listening and public diplomacy. In K.R. Place (Ed.). *Organizational Listening for Strategic Communication Building Theory and Practice*. Routledge. https://doi.org/10.4324/9781003273851-20

Tam, L., Kim, S., & Hutchings, H. (2023). Why are organizations criticized for not listening? Findings from practitioners and stakeholders. In *Organizational Listening for Strategic Communication*, pp. 121–139. Routledge. https://doi.org/10.4324/9781003273851-10

Tannen, D. (1982). Introduction. In D. Tannen (Ed.). *Spoken and Written language: Exploring Orality and Literacy*. Praeger. https://doi.org/10.1007/978-1-4615-9302-7_3

Taylor, M., & Kent, M.L. (2014). Dialogic engagement: Clarifying foundational concepts. *Journal of Public Relations Research, 26*(5), 384–398. https://doi.org/10.1080/1062726X.2014.956106

UAE Embassy (n.d.). *UAE culture*. www.uae-embassy.org/discover-uae/traveling-in-the-uae/uae-culture

UAE Government Portal (n.d., a). *Fact sheet*. https://u.ae/en/about-the-uae/fact-sheet

UAE Government Portal (n.d., b). *The UAE soft power strategy*. https://u.ae/en/about-the-uae/strategies-initiatives-and-awards/strategies-plans-and-visions/strategies-plans-and-visions-untill-2021/the-uae-soft-power-strategy

UAE Government Portal (n.d., c). *Culture*. https://u.ae/en/about-the-uae/culture

UAE Government Portal (n.d., d). *Media regulation*. https://u.ae/en/media/media-in-the-uae/media-regulation

Vakil, S., & Quilliam, N. (2023). *The Abraham Accords and Israel–UAE normalization: Shaping a new Middle East*. Chatham House. www.chathamhouse.org/2023/03/abraham-accords-and-israel-uae-normalization

UAE Ministry of Foreign Affairs (n.d.). *The UAE – facts and figures*. www.mofa.gov.ae/en/the-uae/facts-and-figures.

Valentini, C., Kruckeberg, D., & Starck, K. (2016). The global society and its impact on public relations theorizing: Reflections on major macro trends.

Central European Journal of Communication, 9(2), 229–246. https://doi.org/10.19195/1899-5101.9.2(17).6

Zaharna, R. (1995). Understanding cultural preferences of Arab communication patterns. *Public Relations Review, 21*(3), 241–255. https://doi.org/10.1016/0363-8111(95)90024-1

Zaharna, R.S. (2010). The associative perspective of communication and relational communication in the Arab world. In *Proceedings of Intercultural Competence Conference*, *1*, pp. 398–423. http://cercll.arizona.edu/ICConference2010

Zaharna, R.S. (2016). Beyond the individualism-collectivism divide to relationalism: Explicating cultural assumptions in the concept of "relationships". *Communication Theory, 26*(2), 190–211. https://doi.org/10.1111/comt.12058

Zaharna, R.S. (2022). *Boundary spanners of humanity: Three logics of communications and public diplomacy for global collaboration.* Oxford University Press. https://doi.org/10.1093/oso/9780190930271.001.0001

Zayani, M. (2008). Arab media, corporate communications, and public relations: The case of Al Jazeera. *Asian Journal of Communication, 18*(3), 207–222. https://doi.org/10.1080/01292980802207074

5 On engagement

Bounded relational engagement amid relational dialectics

Ganga S. Dhanesh

Abstract

This chapter explores the impact of cultural factors on the notion of engagement among organizations and publics in the United Arab Emirates (UAE). Specifically, it explores how features of a political economy led by a strong government, a societal culture predominantly underpinned by relational logic, and a media system that operates within restricted freedom of expression impacts the enactment of engagement. Considering the impact of these factors, this chapter proposes the concept of *bounded relational engagement* defined as complex, dialectical connections among interacting entities that are grounded in close, high-quality, interpersonal relationships and networks of homophily, but are simultaneously constrained or hemmed by the inequities created by these hierarchical, networked relationships, and legal, regulatory, and cultural frameworks governing freedom of expression and other boundaries. To illustrate, the chapter discusses a campaign from the UAE, #MakeupForThePay_Gap. While the notion of *bounded relational engagement* reflects specifics of the cultural factors of the UAE, this concept might also be applicable to other contexts that share similar characteristics.

Engagement among organizations and publics

Engagement has been a key concept in public relations research and practice, alongside concepts such as dialogue and relationships (Dhanesh, 2017; Johnston & Taylor, 2018; Morehouse & Saffer, 2023). Popularized in practice, the concept of engagement has received substantial attention from public relations researchers, who have

DOI: 10.4324/9781003368366-5

been investigating engagement from a wide variety of perspectives. However, multiple reviews of the literature on engagement have highlighted not only the lack of a widely accepted conceptualization (Dhanesh, 2017; Morehouse & Saffer, 2019; 2020) but also the lack of a definition that reflects the influence of diverse cultural factors (Marschlich & Ingenhoff, 2021; Zaharna, 2018).

Highlighting the wide variety of definitions of engagement within public relations research, Johnston and Taylor (2018) listed 27 definitions that authors used in their edited volume, the *Handbook of Communication Engagement*. While there is no apparent consensus among scholars, most definitions of engagement within public relations research equate it with communicative interactions among organizations and publics straddling aspects of consultation, listening, involvement, openness, and dialogue (Dhanesh, 2017). For instance, The Encyclopedia of Public Relations' entry titled "Engagement (Stakeholders)" posited, "Public relations is founded on the principle that engagement requires an understanding of and dialogue with stakeholders." Further stressing the connection between engagement and dialogue, Taylor and Kent (2014) placed the notion of engagement within dialogue, particularly its dimension of *propinquity*, which refers to an organization's openness to interacting with, and consulting publics in a timely and relevant manner. According to them, "engagement is part of dialogue and through engagement, organizations and publics can make decisions that create social capital" (p. 384). O'Byrne and Daymon (2014) also offered a definition wherein stakeholder engagement involves "consultation, dialogue, and exchange with the intention of enabling cooperation, increasing understanding, and providing a mechanism for stakeholder involvement in policy-making and decision making" (p. 456). Similarly, practitioners were found to employ engagement strategies, ranging from one-way dissemination of messages to strategies that approached engagement as sense-making towards building and maintaining relationships using dialogue (Kim & Kim, 2015).

While most definitions of public/stakeholder engagement are based on communicative processes of consultation, dialogue, involvement, and open and ethical communication among the interacting entities (Gregory, 2004; Kim & Kim, 2015; O'Byrne & Daymon, 2014; Taylor & Kent, 2014), others have treated public engagement as more than a communicative concept. For instance, Kang (2014) defined public engagement as "a psychologically motivated affective state that brings voluntary extra-role behaviors, and is characterized by affective commitment, positive affectivity and empowerment that an individual public experiences in interactions with an organization over time" (p. 402). This definition added an affective aspect to definitions of public engagement, similar to definitions within the field of employee engagement that has drawn from theories in psychology and organizational behavior to create conceptualizations of employee engagement with three dimensions: cognitive, affective, and behavioral (Kang & Sung, 2017; Karanges et al., 2015; Jiang & Shen, 2023; Men, 2012; Welch, 2011). For instance, Karanges et al. (2015) defined employee engagement as "a positive, fulfilling, work-related state of mind" (p. 129). Similarly, according to Welch (2011), organization engagement is "a dynamic, changeable psychological state, which links employees to their organizations, manifest in organization member role performances expressed physically, cognitively and emotionally, and influenced by organization-level internal communication" (p. 337).

In addition to research on public/stakeholder engagement and employee engagement, public relations scholars have also produced a substantial corpus of work on digital engagement. Although even within this body of work on digital engagement, engagement has been treated as communicative interaction, manifested as clicks, likes, views, shares, comments, tweets, recommendations, and other user-generated content (Jiang et al., 2016; Men & Tsai, 2013; 2014), a few attempts have been made at unshackling definitions of engagement from communicative interaction online. For instance, Yang and Kang (2009) conceptualized and operationalized blog engagement based on cognitive, attitudinal, and behavioral dimensions. Similarly, Bowen (2013) adopted a relational organizational perspective, going beyond clicks, likes, and tweets, and defined digital engagement as "an organization creating active and interested relationships with publics using Internet channels, such as product endorsements by prominent bloggers" (p. 119).

Critiquing the widespread conceptualization of engagement as communicative, without adequately addressing cognitive and affective aspects of engagement, or acknowledging the nonbehavioral aspects of engagement; and the tendency to reify engagement as collaboration over engagement as control, Dhanesh (2017) proposed an alternative definition of engagement as "an affective, cognitive, and behavioral state wherein publics and organizations who share mutual interests in salient topics interact along continua that range from passive to active and from control to collaboration, and is aimed at goal attainment, adjustment, and adaptation for both publics and organizations" (p. 931). In another attempt to consolidate diverse approaches to engagement, Johnston and Taylor (2018) identified three main themes in the definitions presented in the *Handbook of Communication Engagement:* (1) the social and relational focus of engagement, (2) engagement as interaction and exchange, and (3) the dynamic and multidimensional nature of engagement. Reflecting these themes, they proposed three tiers of measuring engagement. Tier 1, or the lowest level of engagement and measurement, indicates that communication activity is present and can be measured by counts and amounts, clicks, and visits. Tier 2, a middle level of engagement, measures connections and relationships at the individual level of analysis. This tier has the strongest association with relationship theorizing in public relations, by including measurement metrics of relationship indices, such as trust, legitimacy, and satisfaction, and measuring interaction quality by interaction outcomes such as long-term cognitive/affective or behavioral outcomes. Tier 3, the highest level of engagement, goes beyond an individual level of analysis and is measured by action and impact at a social level of analysis, including civic indicators such as social capital and participation by disempowered or silent groups in community-based programs. Building off these three tiers of interactive, relational, and societal measurements of engagement, Morehouse and Saffer (2023) proposed the Integrated Network Model of Engagement, highlighting the role of social networks in engagement processes.

However, most of this literature has been generated predominantly in Euro-American contexts of practice, which assumes a robust communicative environment, where organizations and stakeholders communicatively wrangle with each other. How about those contexts which might not share similar characteristics? Zaharna (2018) argued that in order to engage publics globally, "one needs an expansive vision of "engagement" that spans multiple understandings of what makes engagement meaningful to different publics around the world" (p. 313). Offering the example of the United States' low public favorability in the Muslim world despite concerted U.S. public diplomacy efforts post-9/11, Zaharna (2018) posited that the problem was more than using diverse communication strategies but was due to perceptual differences between U.S. public diplomacy and the publics, reflecting relational premises that underlie notions of engagement. Scholars have begun to investigate diverse manifestations of engagement in various contexts across the world (Benmoussa et al., 2023; Marschlich & Ingenhoff, 2021; Zaharna, 2018). While these studies offer various approaches to engagement mostly consistent with extant literature, Zaharna (2018) argued that three distinct yet coexisting relational premises, fundamental to all human societies, may shape logics of engagement: individual, relational, and holistic.

Engagement in the first logic, the individual logic, is grounded in the relational premise of individual autonomy or the absence of relations. As a result, the emphasis is placed on the individual and their efforts to establish relations with others. Features of engagement in the individual logic revolve around classic elements of the public relations planning process, such as source, message, medium, audience, and goal orientation and evaluation. Engagement in the second communication logic, the relational logic, is based on the relational belief that individuals are inherently interconnected. It assumes that connection, rather than separateness or opposition, is the fundamental nature of human relations. Engagement in the relational logic revolves around elements that strengthen and maintain relational ties, such as the importance of personal contact points and connections, physical co-presence that are managed through face-to-face conversations, and nonverbal cues, emotion that serves a binding function in relationships, perspective taking, and symbolism. Engagement in the third communication logic, the holistic logic, shifts from the dyadic focus of the relational logic to a broader, more inclusive perspective that includes all relations. Within this approach, engagement is grounded in the understanding that individuals exist within a complex, preestablished relational structure. Because this structure is based on interconnections among multiple others, engagement in the holistic logic includes the foundational elements of the relational logic—such as contact, nonverbal communication, emotion, perspective-taking, and symbolism—and introduces additional factors essential for preserving the integrity of the whole system. These new elements focus on maintaining harmony and balance among the diverse components of the relational structure and include an expansive view of relations, which are interpenetrating, interconnected, and diverse. Further, processes of synchrony and synergy enable the maintenance and integration of diverse individuals through shared activity and emotion. Engagement in the holistic logic is based on the relational premise that individuals are integral parts of a broader relational network and meaningful engagement involves being attuned to how diverse elements interact and contribute to the whole, ensuring balance and harmony.

Zaharna (2018) argued that while the relational premises make each logic distinctive, the three logics are not mutually exclusive or geoculturally specific. The relational forms (individual, paired dyad, and relational constellation) and salient features (e.g., messages, emotions, synchrony) are inherent in all human societies. Messages and mediated communication are not exclusive to the individual logic, just as emotions are not exclusive to the relational logic. Hence, we can expect the coexistence of the three logics, their related forms, and features at play in a deeply diverse society such as the UAE.

Cultural factors and organization-public engagement in the UAE

Although this chapter will focus on the impact of the UAE's political economy, societal culture, and media culture on the enactment of engagement, it is important to keep in mind that the five factors in the GPRF are interconnected and will be influenced by one another.

Political economy: Strong government and a thriving economy

Although basic information on the UAE's political system has been discussed in Chapter 4, this section will highlight aspects of the political economy that are pertinent to discussing the concept of engagement in the UAE. A nation's political system is often closely associated with its economic system, leading to the term "political economy." According to the GPRF, a pluralistic political system fosters greater economic freedom, which in turn increases competition among economic players (Sriramesh & Vercic, 2009; 2019). This heightened competition often creates a demand for strategic public relations to win public approval and support. However, in economies dominated by monopolistic public sector enterprises, not only does the government wield significant power over private sector companies, including multinational companies, but it also becomes the primary audience for public relations professionals (Dhanesh & Duthler, 2019; Marschlich & Ingenhoff, 2021).

The UAE's economic system is increasingly characterized by a dynamic blend of oil-driven wealth and intense diversification, driven by a mix of state-owned enterprises, multinational corporations, and innovative local startups. Historically reliant on oil exports, the country has made significant strides in diversifying its economy, centered on sectors such as tourism, finance, real estate, and technology. The government has invested heavily in infrastructure, creating airports, ports, and urban developments, and attracting foreign direct investments through initiatives such as Vision 2021 and 2030, aiming for sustainable growth, innovation, and economic resilience, aiming to establish the UAE's soft power in a tumultuous region (UAE Government, 2022). This multi-faceted landscape includes brands such as Emirates, DP World, multinationals such as Unilever and Procter & Gamble, alongside a rising number of homegrown labels catering to a variety of market segments, from luxury consumers to tech-savvy millennials. The emirates of Dubai and Abu Dhabi, in particular, are becoming hubs for regional and global trade and finance. The UAE's economic players target a broad range of audiences, spanning high-net-worth individuals, expatriates, and a growing young demographic, often tailoring products and services to fit cultural preferences and modern aspirations.

Alongside economic growth, the government has set ambitious sustainability goals, hosting the 28th United Nations Climate Change Conference, COP28, in 2023. Companies tend to follow suit with corporate social responsibility (CSR) and sustainability initiatives to engage with key government stakeholders and local communities (Duthler & Dhanesh, 2018; Marschlich & Ingenhoff, 2021; Nickerson & Georgiadou, 2024). While some social issues, such as sexual orientation, might be taboo due to local laws and cultural mores, companies tend to address social issues such as women's empowerment, which also fits with the government's focus on the subject (Khalil & Dhanesh, 2020; Marschlich & Ingenhoff, 2021). Public relations could be a force for social impact in monarchical environments and engage in corporate activism by highlighting the plight of the marginalized through corporate advocacy campaigns (Allagui, 2017). However, it is important to note that all the campaigns analyzed by Allagui (2017) dealt with topics such as children with special needs and spreading happiness among low-income workers, which do not violate the unwritten rules of topics companies can and cannot engage with. How does the notion of stakeholder engagement fit in with the particularities of the UAE's political economy, especially with a strong government that owns or has substantial control over many nonprofit organizations and local companies and a thriving economic scene filled with public and private sector, local and multinational players?

First, examining engagement through the lens of corporate diplomacy of multinational companies in the UAE, Marschlich and Ingenhoff (2021) found that corporate diplomacy, specifically relating to social issues, relies heavily on engagement with governmental entities. The government is the primary stakeholder, and collaborating with it is necessary to gain access to other influential actors and private citizens. Engagement with the government is key because it also improves the credibility of foreign companies operating in the UAE. However, they noted that because the government also relies on partnerships with MNCs to achieve social and sustainability goals at a national level, the MNCs' engagement with the government was seen as mutually beneficial.

Second, Badran (2017) has reported on governmental initiatives of online citizen engagement, aimed to "involve the UAE society in government decision-making processes, according them a direct role in influencing government decisions and contributing to government strategies" (p. 118). Given the high level of Internet penetration and social media adoption in the country, the UAE government launched an initiative called "The UAE Brainstorming Session," a technology-driven citizen engagement event that utilized popular social media platforms to gather public input on two under-performing sectors: public health and education. The UAE Prime Minister personally promoted the event via Twitter, leading to the generation of 82,000 ideas from both citizens and residents, all of which were considered by a ministerial committee, and some were subsequently implemented.

While the first instance of corporate diplomacy as engagement appeared to reflect the notion of relational engagement, the second instance of online citizen engagement appeared to reflect definitions of engagement that reify communicative interaction that also contributes to societal impact.

Societal culture: Relationalism and other logics of engagement

Multiple dialectical tensions affect the enactment of stakeholder engagement in the UAE. For instance, Middle Eastern countries, including the UAE, predominantly embrace relational logic (Zaharna, 2018), reflected in the high value ascribed to relationships (AlSaqer & Al Hashimi, 2019) and in Arab values that accord much importance to social interaction and serving society (Al-Kandari & Gaither, 2011; AlSaqer & Al Hashimi, 2019). These factors ought to provide favorable conditions for stakeholder engagement processes. However, Islamic values also reflect adherence to hierarchy (AlSaqer & Al Hashimi, 2019), which could complicate stakeholder engagement processes. How do these tensions affect the enactment of stakeholder engagement in the UAE?

Marschlich and Ingenhoff (2021) found the importance of high-quality, close relationships for successful corporate diplomacy engagement in the UAE. Without building good relationships, especially with governmental entities and their acquaintances, MNCs cannot get involved in decision-making or get invited to government-led forums where critical issues are discussed and decisions made. In the context of discussing relationships, they also highlighted the importance of social networks (Morehouse & Saffer, 2023). The importance of networks in engagement processes reflects the notion of contact points or personal connections, which underlies the indigenous Arab social network structure of *wasta* (Valk et al., 2024; Zaharna, 2018). *Wasta* is a pervasive cultural construct in Arab countries that constitutes an exclusive familial, social, informal network of relationships, which often reflect deeply embedded societal structures (Ali & Weir, 2020; Horak, 2022). Network members enjoy strong social ties, cohesion, and loyalty, reflecting features of homophily, and receive preferential treatment from members who wield power or authority (Ali & Weir, 2020; Horak, 2022; Morehouse & Saffer, 2023). However, personal networks of influence also emphasize "the cold nature of social inequalities" that reflect the adage "it's not what you know, it's who you know" (Garcia, 2024, p. 89).

The idea of stakeholder engagement through close relationships and networks is predicated on face-to-face communication and physical co-presence (Marschlich & Ingenhoff, 2021; Zaharna, 2018). In physical spaces where stakeholder engagement happens, nonverbal behavior is paramount in defining and maintaining relationships by providing cues in gauging trust or power (Zaharna, 2018). In addition to stakeholder engagement through networks, scholars have highlighted the importance of personal matters in stakeholder engagement and relationship building (Derrick, 2023; Marschlich &

Ingenhoff, 2021). For example, in *Majlis* meetings, an informal participatory system of public consultation where citizens can interact with rulers to share their opinions and concerns, personal relationships are pivotal as business issues are discussed after talking about their personal lives, especially family life. Marschlich and Ingenhoff (2021) found that building close, personal relationships with decision-makers strengthened the engagement process for MNCs. One of the downsides of the importance of personal and patronage relationships to the practice of public relations in most parts of the world is how open or closed the public sphere is to a variety of stakeholders (Garcia, 2024). As Garcia (2024) pointed out, "… in models that rely heavily on interpersonal relationships, the practice of public relations is paradoxically more private" (p.91).

In addition to highlighting the importance of building close, personal relationships with key governmental actors, Marschlich and Ingenhoff (2021) found that MNCs in the UAE also considered corporate diplomacy as community engagement, wherein they leveraged their commitment to social and environmental issues in the country to generate a social license to operate through relationship cultivation with citizens. Civic engagement processes were also similarly built through events that allowed for face-to-face conversations and dialogue with citizens.

Although this chapter has been discussing characteristics of relational logic so far, the UAE also hosts a diverse population, with around 90 percent of the population being expatriates. This implies that multiple engagement strategies suited for individual, relational, and holistic logics are needed simultaneously that engage with diverse communication patterns found in an extremely diverse society (Marschlich & Ingenhoff, 2021; Zaharna, 2018).

Media: Calibrated expression

While physical co-presence through face-to-face conversations is critical for stakeholder engagement in the cultural context of the UAE, mediated engagement processes are also on the rise, particularly through influencer relations. Research has also examined the use of online media for citizen engagement and engagement for nonprofit organizations.

According to a 2023 study on the state of influencer marketing in the UAE, 76.9% of marketers said that Influencer Marketing is a top priority for their brand, second only to the use of social media. 71.8% of respondents said that they measure the success of their Influencer Marketing campaign through engagement, measured by likes, comments, and shares (YAAP & Khaleej Times, 2023). Given that trust in influencers can have downstream effects on the organizations they represent, influencer transparency in declaring paid endorsements can positively influence the influencer–follower relationship, purchase intention, and electronic word-of-mouth intention in the UAE (Dhanesh & Duthler, 2019).

Reflecting the trend across Arab countries to leverage social media for citizen engagement, in the UAE too, the government has been making strides in engaging citizens and residents through social media (Badran, 2017). Although traditionally the UAE has employed the *Majlis* for public consultation, the UAE government's citizenship engagement initiative described earlier was aptly described as "From Majlis to Hashtag: The rise of digital citizen engagement in the UAE" in a 2014 report by the Dubai-based Mohammed Bin Rashid School of Government, in partnership with the UAE Ministry of Cabinet Affairs (Badran, 2017).

However, due to stringent media laws discussed earlier in Chapter 4, there is a lack of freedom of expression and public opinion in the UAE (Kirat, 2005), which complicates engagement processes because companies are often ignorant about what community members think about social issues and what they expect from companies (Marschlich & Ingenhoff, 2021).

Yet another strand of research has considered nonprofit organizations' online engagement with their stakeholders. These studies have found that the use of social media by nonprofit organizations is marked by a strong control over discourse and low affective involvement, which undermines their ability to effectively engage stakeholders on social media (Ben Moussa et al., 2023; Ben Moussa & Benmessaoud, 2021).

Stakeholder engagement in a context with strong government leadership, relationalism, and calibrated digital media: Proposing *bounded relational engagement*

The description of the UAE's political economy, societal, and media cultures has highlighted a context for stakeholder engagement that is different from contexts where wrangling in the marketplace of ideas is more commonly assumed. Factors such as a strong government that aims for soft power leadership through multiple avenues, including leadership on sustainability matters, ensure that the government is the key stakeholder in engagement processes of multinational companies who seek to gain societal legitimacy and credibility through their corporate diplomacy and sustainability efforts. The predominant cultural infrastructure of relationalism implies that corporate engagement efforts become successful only when close personal relationships and networks are established with key social actors, including governmental entities. Finally, the legal bounds on freedom of expression and public opinion in the UAE complicate engagement processes because companies are often in the dark about what their stakeholders think and expect of companies. How do these factors affect the conceptualization of public/stakeholder engagement in the UAE? How does the concept of engagement as embedded in predominantly individual logics of public relations fit the largely relational logics of the Middle East, further complicated by the presence of a diverse expatriate community in the UAE that might engage with relational premises fundamental to individual, relational, and holistic logics?

This chapter argues that the notion of stakeholder engagement in extant public relations literature needs to shape shift to fit these cultural factors specific to the UAE. I do this by basing it on Zaharna's notion of relationalism (2018), existing definitions in public relations that build on relationalism (Garcia, 2024; Johnson & Taylor, 2018), and the importance of networks in engagement processes (Morehouse & Saffer, 2023). I propose the concept of *bounded relational engagement*, defined as complex, dialectical connections among interacting entities that are grounded in close, high-quality, interpersonal relationships and networks of homophily, but are simultaneously constrained or nudged by the inequities created by these hierarchical, networked relationships, and legal, regulatory, and cultural frameworks governing freedom of expression and other boundaries.

This definition highlights the dialectical tensions that energize engagement processes in the UAE. The preeminence of close, high-quality interpersonal relationships and social networks based on homophily can strengthen engagement processes, leading to outcomes at the individual, organizational, and societal levels, including indicators of relational quality such as trust and creation of social capital. However, in contexts with strong governmental control and regulatory and cultural restrictions on freedom of expression, engagement occurs through indirect channels, relying on established connections and the subtleties of personal influence rather than open dialogue in the public sphere. Relying on interpersonal, networked relationships also highlights the importance of navigating the power dynamics embedded in hierarchical relationships and social networks, thus making engagement bounded by the inequities embedded in networked, hierarchical relational constellations. Taken together, the concept of *bounded relational engagement* is a dialectical concept that reflects a complex panoply of factors that characterize engagement in the UAE. While this definition reflects the specifics of the political economy, societal, and media cultures of the UAE, it might also be applicable to other contexts that share similar characteristics.

To illustrate this conceptualization of engagement in the UAE, I next discuss a campaign from the UAE, #MakeupForThePay_Gap.

Case study: #MakeupForThePay_Gap

This case study is on a public relations campaign, #MakeupForThePay_Gap, which was shortlisted under the social engagement and influencer marketing category at the 2024 Dubai Lynx, the premier festival of creativity in the region, a sister festival to Cannes Lions. The organization was ItsHerWay.com, a leading female entrepreneur network in the UAE whose mission is to "empower women entrepreneurs to build successful businesses by providing them with resources, connections, and opportunities. We envision a world where women-led businesses thrive, supported by a strong network of fellow women entrepreneurs, mentors, and partners" (www.itsherway.com/pages/about-us). The concept and art direction were by the agency Leo Burnett, Dubai.

According to the campaign brief, across the world, women get paid 23% less than men, a gender pay gap that increases to 54% in the MENA region. Although one of the most effective ways is for women to demand equal pay, given the region's male-dominated workforce and patriarchal culture, this would be seen as being aggressive, demanding, or difficult. ItsHerWay leveraged the insight that makeup tutorials are one of the most-watched content on social media by women in the region's workforce. They partnered with the region's most followed makeup influencers to launch makeup tutorials with a purpose on TikTok, where this content is most commonly consumed. The tutorial began like any other ordinary makeup tutorial but then progressed into showing the influencers using makeup to transform into men, with the influencer demonstrating how to "brush your eyebrows to get that bushy, masculine look" so that you can achieve the "perfect makeup look to get you that important promotion or to help you with some workplace validation." The video ended with the fact that over 1.6 billion women worldwide would get paid more had they been men and invited viewers to take up the challenge. #MakeupForThePay_Gap became the top trending topic and hashtag on TikTok with over 13.2 million views and over 25K likes in the first week of launching the campaign. The tutorials resonated with a high uptake of the #MakeupForThePay_Gap filter and user-generated content. In addition to the video, ItsHerWay also hosted the region's first Equal Pay Conference, where companies from across the region were invited to take a pledge against this gender bias and to become equal-pay employers.

In this case study, quite a few aspects of *bounded relational engagement* are evident. First off, the topic of the gender pay gap fits in with the government's prioritization of women empowerment in the country. While this is an important issue, it fits in nicely with the boundaries of social issues organizations can engage with in the country, without pushing the envelope with related issues such as LGBTQ rights. Second, although the campaign itself leveraged the popular strategy of engaging influencers for an online TikTok campaign, the organization itself is predicated on the connections, networks, and relationships among the community of women entrepreneurs in the country, bonded by networks of homophily. The campaign also melds message appeal strategies that leverage facts and emotions, in a nod to appealing to different communication strategies that might appeal to the diverse communities in the country who might resonate more with individual, relational, and holistic logics. The outcome metrics showed that these strategies paid off in terms of interactive engagement.

Questions for further discussion

1 In addition to features of the political economy, societal, and media cultures, what other cultural factors might affect stakeholder engagement in diverse cultural contexts?
2 How might the concept of *Bounded Relational Engagement* change in response to the influence of other cultural factors in the GPRF?
3 Do you think multinational companies face additional challenges in establishing engagement processes in host countries when compared to local companies?

4 How can multinational companies design systems and processes of engagement in different countries, while meeting requirements for engagement in their home country?
5 Can you think of an example where engagement processes that reflected or did not reflect cultural factors had a deep impact on the interacting entities?

References

Ali, S., & Weir, D. (2020). Wasta: Advancing a holistic model to bridge the micro- macro divide. *Management and Organization Review, 16*(3), 657–685. https://doi.org/10.1017/mor.2020.27

Al-Kandari, A., & Gaither, T.K. (2011). Arabs, the west and public relations: A critical/cultural study of Arab cultural values. *Public Relations Review, 37*(3), 266–273. https://doi.org/10.1016/j.pubrev.2011.04.002

Allagui, I. (2017). Towards organizational activism in the UAE: A case study approach. *Public Relations Review*, *43*, 258–266. https://doi.org/10.1016/j.pubrev.2016.12.007

AlSaqer, L., & Al Hashimi, S. (2019). The status and new directions of public relations practice in Bahrain. In T. M. Almutairi and D. Kruckeberg (Eds.). *Public Relations in the Gulf Cooperation Countries: An Arab Perspective* (pp. 5–30). Routledge. https://doi.org/10.4324/9781351064989-2

Badran, B.A. (2017). Strategic communication and public engagement: The UAE e-brainstorming session. *Asian Journal of Media and Communication, 1*(2), 113–122. https://doi.org/10.20885/asjmc.vol1.iss2.art2

Benmoussa, M., & Benmessaoud, S. (2021). Online engagement as a multimodal discursive practice: The case of Dubai Cares' Facebook page. *Public Relations Inquiry, 10*(1), 49–71. https://doi.org/10.1177/2046147X20979291

Benmoussa, M., Zaid, B., & Ayad, K. (2023). Non-profit organizations' online engagement and the limits of charity rhetoric: The case of the United Arab Emirates. *Journal of Nonprofit & Public Sector Marketing, 36*(4), 413–436. https://doi.org/10.1080/10495142.2023.2281905

Bowen, S.A. (2013). Using classic social media cases to distill ethical guidelines for digital engagement. *Journal of Mass Media Ethics, 28*(2), 119–133. https://doi.org/10.1080/08900523.2013.793523

Derrick, S. (2023, October 16). Redefining PR in the Middle East: Strategies, growth, and culture. *PR Week*. www.prweek.com/article/1838953/redefining-pr-middle-east.

Dhanesh, G.S. (2017). Putting engagement in its PRoper place: State of the field, definition and model of engagement in public relations. *Public Relations Review, 43*(5), 925–933. https://doi.org/10.1016/j.pubrev.2017.04.001

Dhanesh, G.S., & Duthler, G. (2019). Relationship management through social media influencers: Effects of followers' awareness of paid endorsement. *Public Relations Review, 45*(3), 101765. https://doi.org/10.1016/j.pubrev.2019.03.002

Duthler, G., & Dhanesh, G.S. (2018). The role of corporate social responsibility (CSR) and its internal communication in predicting employee engagement: Perspectives from the United Arab Emirates (UAE). *Public Relations Review, 44*(4), 453–462. https://doi.org/10.1016/j.pubrev.2018.04.001

Garcia, C. (2024). De-westernizing public relations: A comparative and global perspective on the influence of personal and patronage relationships across the world. *Catalan Journal of Communication and Cultural Studies, 16*(1), 83–99. https://doi.org/10.1386/cjcs_00096_1

Gregory, A. (2004). The ethics of engagement in the UK public sector: A case in point. *Journal of Communication Management, 8*(1), 83–94. https://doi.org/10.1108/13632540410807565

Horak, S. (Ed.). (2022). *Informal Networks in International Business*. Bingley, UK: Emerald Publishing Limited Howard House, Wagon Lane. https://doi.org/10.1108/9781839828782

Jiang, H., Luo, Y., & Kulemeka, O. (2016). Social media engagement as an evaluation barometer: Insights from communication executives. *Public Relations Review, 42*(4), 679–691. https://doi.org/10.1016/j.pubrev.2015.12.004

Jiang, H., & Shen, H. (2023). Toward a relational theory of employee engagement: Understanding authenticity, transparency, and employee behaviors. *International Journal of Business Communication, 60*(3), 948–975. https://doi.org/10.1177/2329488420954236

Johnston, K. A., & Taylor, M. (Eds.). (2018). *The Handbook of Communication Engagement*. Wiley-Blackwell. https://doi.org/10.1002/9781119167600

Kang, M. (2014). Understanding public engagement: Conceptualizing and measuring its influence on supportive behavioral intentions. *Journal of Public Relations Research, 26*(5), 399–416. https://doi.org/10.1080/1062726X.2014.956107

Kang, M., & Sung, M. (2017). How symmetrical employee communication leads to employee engagement and positive employee communication behaviors: The mediation of employee-organization relationships. *Journal of Communication Management, 21*, 82–102. https://doi.org/10.1108/JCOM-04-2016-0026

Karanges, E., Johnston, K., Beatson, A., & Lings, I. (2015). The influence of internal communication on employee engagement: A pilot study. *Public Relations Review, 41*(129), 131. https://doi.org/10.1016/j.pubrev.2014.12.003

Khalil, A. & Dhanesh, G.S. (2020). Gender stereotypes in television advertising in the Middle East: Time for marketers and advertisers to step up.

Business Horizons, 63(5), 671–679. https://doi.org/10.1016/j.bushor.2020.05.004

Kim, S., & Kim, J.-N. (2015). Bridge or buffer: Two ideas of effective corporate governance and public engagement. *Journal of Public Affairs: An International Journal, 16*(2), 118–127. https://doi.org/10.1002/pa.1555

Kirat, M. (2005). Public relations practice in the Arab World: A critical assessment. *Public Relations Review, 31*(3), 323–332. https://doi.org/10.1016/j.pubrev.2005.05.016

Marschlich, S., & Ingenhoff, D. (2021). Stakeholder engagement in a multicultural context: The contribution of (personal) relationship cultivation to social capital. *Public Relations Review, 47*(4), 102091. https://doi.org/10.1016/j.pubrev.2021.102091

Men, L.R. (2012). CEO credibility, perceived organizational reputation, and employee engagement. *Public Relations Review, 38*(1), 171–173. https://doi.org/10.1016/j.pubrev.2011.12.011

Men, L.R., & Tsai, W.-H. (2013). Beyond liking or following: Understanding public engagement on social networking sites in China. *Public Relations Review*, *39*, 13–22. https://doi.org/10.1016/j.pubrev.2012.09.013

Men, L.R., & Tsai, W.-H. (2014). Perceptual, attitudinal, and behavioral outcomes of organization-public engagement on corporate social networking sites. *Journal of Public Relations Research, 26*(5), 417–435. https://doi.org/10.1080/1062726X.2014.951047

Morehouse, J., & Saffer, A.J. (2019). Illuminating the invisible college: An analysis of foundational and prominent publications of engagement research in public relations. *Public Relations Review, 45*(5), 101836. https://doi.org/10.1016/j.pubrev.2019.101836

Morehouse, J., & Saffer, A.J. (2020). The knowledge construction network of engagement research: Examining scholars' star collaborators, embeddedness, and influence. *Public Relations Review, 46*(3), 101924. https://doi.org/10.1016/j.pubrev.2020.101924

Morehouse, J., & Saffer, A.J. (2023). Putting stakeholders' engagement in the equation: Proposing the integrated network engagement model. *Public Relations Review, 49*(1), 102291. https://doi.org/10.1016/j.pubrev.2023.102291

Nickerson, C. & Georgiadou, E., (2024). Actioning and promoting corporate social responsibility initiatives: A focus on the United Arab Emirates. *Strategic Direction, 40*(9), 7–9. https://doi.org/10.1108/SD-09-2024-0160

O'Byrne, S., & Daymon, C. (2014). Irresponsible engagement and the citizen investor. *Journal of Public Relations Research, 26*(5), 455–473. https://doi.org/10.1080/1062726X.2014.956105

Taylor, M., & Kent, M.L. (2014). Dialogic engagement: Clarifying foundational concepts. *Journal of Public Relations Research, 26*(5), 384–398. https://doi.org/10.1080/1062726X.2014.956106

UAE Government (2022). *The UAE soft power strategy*. UAE Government. https://u.ae/en/about-the-uae/strategies-initiatives-and-awards/strategies-plans-and-visions/strategies-plans-and-visions-untill-2021/the-uae-soft-power-strategy

Valk, R., Yousif, L., & McGarvey, L. (2024). Exploring Wasta and religious values and principles: A case study of employee engagement in the UAE hospitality sector. *Arab Economic and Business Journal, 16*(1), Article 2. https://doi.org/10.38039/2214-4625.1039

Welch, M. (2011). The evolution of the employee engagement concept: Communication implications. *Corporate Communications: An International Journal, 16*(4), 328–346. https://doi.org/10.1108/13563281111186968

YAAP & Khaleej Times (2023). *Influence: The state of influencer marketing in the UAE*.

Yang, S.-U., & Kang, M. (2009). Measuring blog engagement: Testing a four-dimensional scale. *Public Relations Review, 35*(3), 323–324. https://doi.org/10.1016/j.pubrev.2009.05.004

Zaharna, R.S. (2018). Global engagement: Culture and communication insights from public diplomacy. In K.A. Johnston and M. Taylor (Eds.). *The Handbook of Communication Engagement*. Wiley-Blackwell. https://doi.org/10.1002/9781119167600.ch21

Concluding remarks

The way forward for intercultural public relations

Ruth Avidar and Ganga S. Dhanesh

This book started by noting the Euro-American-centeredness of theorizing in public relations research despite the historical origins, and current levels of growth and maturity of the public relations profession across the world. Even the extant body of knowledge on global public relations has been critiqued for applying dominant theories from clusters of Western-centric strategic management research to non-Western contexts, because the underpinning ideologies of individualism, democracy, marketization, consumption, and self-promotion characteristic of Western values might not automatically transfer to non-Western contexts. This theoretical imperialism is also reflected in public relations education across the world due to the widespread adoption of U.S. public relations textbooks. Further, scholars have critiqued the functionalist, normative, management-centric tendencies of public relations research that propagate Western modernist, functionalist ideologies and have urged public relations researchers to undertake the challenging but important work of representing contours of diverse practice from across the world. Subsequently, the critical-cultural turn in public relations research employed lenses of postmodernism (Holtzhausen, 2011), critical modernism (Pal & Dutta, 2008), and postcolonialism (Dutta & Pal, 2011) to study public relations practice in diverse regions.

However, the critical-cultural paradigm has been criticized for "an overwhelming determinism that paralyzes actual practice," while the postmodern paradigm "lends itself to a situational relativism that can be equally paralyzing" (Curtin & Gaither, 2005, p. 95). In response, this book aimed to straddle both the macro and micro approaches by (a) adopting the macro variables of the GPRF, including political,

DOI: 10.4324/9781003368366-6

economic, societal, organizational, media, and activist cultures, while (b) delving into micro cultural variables relevant to the Middle Eastern countries, to offer insights into intercultural public relations that reflect the finer nuances of practice situated within specific cultural mores. We asked how political, economic, societal, organizational, activist, and media cultures influence the practice of public relations in the Middle East.

We examined the enactment of four key public relations concepts in the Middle East, specifically in Israel and the UAE. While Ruth Avidar examined the concepts of organizational identity and reputation in Israel, Ganga Dhanesh dealt with the enactment of organizational listening and engagement in the UAE. These concepts were chosen because they are some of the key concepts in public relations practice that we thought might be impacted the most by cultural factors. The four chapters examined the influence of various interconnected variables of the GPRF on the enactment of these concepts and illustrated these culturally specific nuances with case study examples.

Ruth Avidar introduced the concept of *culturally grounded organizational identity formation* to address the dynamic, co-creational processes through which organizations construct their identities in response to socio-political, economic, and cultural realities. She also proposed the *culturally embedded organizational reputation model*, which identifies cultural integration and responsiveness, political and economic adaptability, media savviness, and co-creation and meaningful engagement with stakeholders as critical factors in building organizational reputation.

Ganga Dhanesh proposed the concept of *subtextual organizational listening* as appropriate to organizational listening in a high context, indirect, oral culture with a regulated media system. She also proposed the concept of *bounded relational engagement* defined as complex, dialectical connections among interacting entities that are grounded in close, high-quality, interpersonal relationships and networks of homophily, but are simultaneously constrained by the inequities created by these hierarchical, networked relationships, and legal, regulatory, and cultural frameworks.

Both authors argued that while these frameworks and concepts have been generated in culturally specific contexts of practice in Israel and the UAE, they can be applied in other contexts with similar characteristics. These four chapters, which straddled both the macro GPRF and micro cultural variables relevant to the specific countries under study, offer a template that can be used in exploring the influence of cultural factors on the enactment of key public relations concepts in diverse cultural contexts. It is our hope that this attempt at trying to reduce the deeply rooted ethnocentricity of public relations research (Rechavi et al., 2024) will be replicated by others in diverse regions of the world. For instance, more work can be done on public relations practice across the African continent that attends to indigenous cultures' ancient philosophies as called for by Pompper and Adae (2022). Perhaps studies can examine the influence of diverse political, economic, societal, organizational, media, and activist cultures on the practice of key public relations concepts in various countries in Africa. The same can be extended to underexamined regions of the world including South and Southeast Asia.

References

Curtin, P.A., & Gaither, T.K. (2005). Privileging identity, difference, and power: The circuit of culture as a basis for public relations theory. *Journal of Public Relations Research*, *17*(2), 91–115.

Dutta, M.J., & Pal, M. (2011). Public relations and marginalization in a global context: A postcolonial critique. In N. Bardhan, and C.K. Weaver (Eds.). *Public Relations in Global Contexts: Multi-paradigmatic Perspectives*. Routledge.

Holtzhausen, D.R. (2011). The need for a postmodern turn in global public relations. In N. Bardhan and C.K. Weaver (Eds.). *Public Relations in Global Contexts: Multi-paradigmatic Perspectives*, pp. 140–166. Routledge.

Pal, M., & Dutta, M.J. (2008). Public relations in a global context: The relevance of critical modernism as a theoretical lens. *Journal of Public Relations Research*, *20*(2), 159–179. doi:10.1080/10627260801894280

Pompper, D., & Adae, E.K. (2022). PR and Sustainability across the African Continent: Using Afro-Centric philosophies to remember what's been 'forgotten or lost'. Paper Presented at the Annual Conference of the AEJMC.

Rechavi, A., Avidar, R., & Roth-Cohen, O. (2024). Geographical-institutional diversity and heterophily in academic research: a social network analysis of international collaboration, research communities and co-authorship in the public relations discipline. *Atlantic Journal of Communication*, *33*(1), 71–93. https://doi.org/10.1080/15456870.2024.2371463

Index

FSC
www.fsc.org
MIX
Papier | Fördert
gute Waldnutzung
FSC® C083411

Kolibri 360 GmbH
Ferdinand-Jühlke-Straße 7
99095 Erfurt, Deutschland
produktsicherheit@kolibri360.de